Introduction to the Economics and Mathematics of Financial Markets
Solutions Manual

Jakša Cvitanić and Fernando Zapatero

The MIT Press
Cambridge, Massachusetts
London, England

ISBN 0-262-53259-X

10 9 8 7 6 5 4 3 2 1

INTRODUCTION TO THE ECONOMICS AND MATHEMATICS OF FINANCIAL MARKETS: SOLUTIONS MANUAL

Jakša Cvitanić and Fernando Zapatero

September 2003

Table of Contents

INTRODUCTION

This manual contains the solutions to the end-of-the chapters problems in *Introduction to the Economics and Mathematics of Financial Markets* (MIT Press, 2003), that have a † sign, as in **† 14**, when problem 14 is solved in the manual. For some problems for which the main part consists of writing a computer program and doing computations, we only give suggestions and not full solutions. For these, the book web page **http://math.usc.edu/~cvitanic/book.html** contains Microsoft Excel files that can be helpful. The files have names like "ch1.xls". That particular file has all the figures from Chapter 1 of the book, and all the computations needed to produce them. We use only basic features of Excel, except for Monte Carlo simulation for which we use the Visual Basic programming language, incorporated in Excel. At a few places in the book we do give "Excel Tips" that point out what trickier commands have been used. Other, more mathematically oriented software may be more efficient for longer computations such as Monte Carlo simulation, and we leave the choice of the software to be used with some of these to the instructor or the reader.

Please report any errors or suggested corrections to cvitanic@math.usc.edu or zapatero@usc.edu. Corrections will be posted at the book web page.

1 FINANCIAL MARKETS

† 2. How "risk-free" are bonds as financial instruments?

Solution: Bonds are called risk-free (or fixed income) securities because the stream of the cash-flows promised by the issuer until maturity is known in advance. That is, when investors buy bonds, they know the exact amounts and dates of payments. However, that does not make bonds completely risk-free. One reason is, there is a risk of default of the issuer. When the issuer is the U.S. government, the risk of default is considered non-existent. That is the reason why the denomination of "risk-free" securities is typically reserved for government bonds. Another reason is that if the investor decides to sell the bond in the market before maturity, the price will depend on prevailing interest rates at the time of the sale, which cannot be predicted. Still another reason is, even if the investor keeps the bond until maturity, only the nominal value of the payments is known, but not the real value. That is, if there is, for example, high inflation between the moment the investor buys the bond and maturity, the money paid to the investor will have "less value" than if inflation is low.

† 4. Why are stocks usually more risky than bonds?

Solution: Bonds are called risk-free securities because the future stream of payments promised to the holder of the security is known in advance. Nevertheless, as argued in Problem 2, there are some risks when holding bonds. In the case of stocks, not only the same sources of risk are present, but, additionally, it is not known in advance what payments (if any) the stockholder will receive. The firm has to generate enough cash to pay the bondholders and then, if there is any residual left, the stockholders can be compensated, or, which increases the uncertainty, a part of it can be reinvested with the hope of generating higher future earnings.

NOTE: In the problems below, we disregard the interest that may be earned or paid on the money borrowed/lent.

† **6.** Being a sophisticated trader, you are not afraid to engage in selling shares short. You sell short 100 shares of Internet Bust Company, at the market price of $20.00 per share. What is your profit or loss if you exit the short position five months from now and a share of the company is worth $15.00?

Solution: You sold short $100 \cdot 20 = 2,000$ worth of shares. In order to close the short position you have to buy and return $100 \cdot 15 = 1,500$ worth of shares. Your profit is $500. (We disregard the interest that may be earned or paid on the money borrowed/lent.)

† **8.** The company Nice Books International owned by the authors of this book promises to pay you back $50.00 for each copy of the book you buy this year if, five years from now, the book is out of print. For this promise, you have to pay additional $10.00 when buying a copy. If you agree to this proposal, are you buying the company's stock, the company's bond, or a derivative contract?

Solution: It is a derivative contract since the payoff depends on a random outcome.

† **12.** Explain the difference between entering into a short forward contract with the forward price $50.00 and selling a call option with a strike price of $50.00.

Solution: A short forward contract implies the obligation to sell the underlying at a price of $50.00, regardless of the price of the underlying at maturity. It can result in a profit if the underlying is worth less than $50.00 or a loss if the underlying is worth more than $50.00. Moreover, there is no exchange of money at the beginning. When selling a call, the writer (seller) sells the right, but not the obligation to the holder to buy the underlying at maturity for $50.00. The call holder has to pay some money to the writer at the beginning. The call holder will buy the underlying at maturity if the price of the underlying is higher than $50.00, which may result in a loss for the writer, depending on the amount the writer was paid at the beginning. If the price of the underlying at maturity is lower than $50.00, the call holder will not exercise it and the writer's profit is the money he/she was paid at the beginning.

† **14.** You buy a European put option on Up&Down, Inc., stock with maturity $T = 6$ months, and strike price $K = \$54.00$. You pay $1.00 for the option.

a. Suppose that at maturity the stock's market price is $50.00. What is your total profit or loss?

b. What is the profit or loss when at maturity the stock price is $57.00?

Solution: a. You exercise the put option – you can buy the stock for 50.00 and sell it to the writer of the option for 54.00. Since you paid 1.00, your profit is

$$P\&L = 54 - 50 - 1 = \$3.00 \ .$$

b. You don't exercise the option:

$$P\&L = -\$1.00 \ .$$

† 18. At time zero you enter a short position in futures contracts on 20 shares of the stock XYZ at the futures price of $50.00. Moreover, you sell (write) 5 "exotic" options of the following type: they are put options, but using as the underlying asset the average of the today's stock price and the stock price at maturity, rather than using the stock price at maturity as the underlying asset. The option's strike price is $K = \$52.00$, the option selling price today is $5.00 per option and the today's stock price is $S(0) = \$49.00$ per share. The maturity of all of your positions is $T = 2$ months. What is your total profit or loss two months from now if

a. at maturity the price of one stock share is $57.00?

b. at maturity the price of one stock share is $47.00?

Solution: a. You lose $20 \cdot (57 - 50) = 140$ in the forward contract. You receive $5 \cdot 5 = 25$ for the options. Since the average of the initial and the final stock price is 53, the put option is not exercised, that is, you have to pay $5 \cdot (52 - 53)^+ = 0$ as the options payoff. Your total profit or loss is

$$P\&L = -20 \cdot (57 - 50) + 5 \cdot 5 - 0 = -115 \ .$$

b. You gain $20 \cdot (50 - 47) = 60$ from the forward contract. You receive $5 \cdot 5 = 25$ for the options. The average of the initial and the final stock price is 48, the put option is exercised, and you have to pay $5 \cdot (52 - 48)^+ = 20$ as the options payoff. Your total profit or loss is

$$P\&L = 20 \cdot (50 - 47) + 5 \cdot 5 - 5 \cdot (52 - 48)^+ = 65 \ .$$

† 22. You would like to buy $200,000 worth of the stock Good Potential, Inc., but you have only $60,000 to invest. You buy the $200,000 worth at margin. The intermediary requires a maintenance margin of $145,000. Four months from now the value of the total stock purchased falls to $125,000. What is the amount of the margin call the intermediary would send you?

Solution: You will have to deposit assets (cash or other securities) for a total of $145,000-$125,000=$20,000.

2 INTEREST RATES

† 2. A bank quotes the nominal annual rate of 6%, and it compounds interest every two months. What is the value of one dollar deposited in this bank after a year?

Solution: Value $= (1 + r/6)^6 = 1.01^6 = 1.0615$.

† 4. An investment opportunity guarantees total interest of 20% over a period of three years. What is the effective annual rate corresponding to annual compounding?

Solution: We need to have $(1 + r)^3 = 1.2$, or $1 + r = 1.2^{1/3}$. This gives $r = 0.0627$.

† 6. What is the value of $1.00 after 50 days if the continuous annual rate is 10%?

Solution: Value $= e^{0.1 \cdot 50/365} = 1.0138$.

† 10. You are facing two business opportunities with the following cash flows:

a. Investing $10,000 today, receiving $5,000 after three months, $4,500 after six months, and another $4,500 nine months from today.

b. Alternatively, you can invest $11,480 today, and receive $5,500, $5,000 and $5,000 after three, six and nine months.

What is the better investment for you, part a or part b? Assume that the nominal annual rate is 5%, and compounding is done quarterly.

Solution:

a. Present value $= -10000 + 5000/1.0125 + 4500/(1.0125^2) + 4500/(1.0125^3) = 3663.229$.

b. Present value $= -11480 + 5500/1.0125 + 5000/(1.0125^2) + 5000/(1.0125^3) = 3646.496$.

Deal in part a is better.

† 12. Consider the framework of the previous problem. Before you take a loan you compare two banks: Bank A offers a 15-year mortgage loan of $50,000 at the nominal rate of 8.5%, with monthly compounding , with the APR of 9.00%. Bank B offers a 15-year mortgage loan of $50,000 at the nominal rate of 8.8%, with monthly compounding, with the APR of 9.2%. Which bank is charging you more in fees?

Solution: We have $m = 15 \cdot 12 = 180$. For bank A the APR per period is $r = 0.09/12 = 0.0075$. The value of the loan is $V(0) = 50,000$. The monthly payment is

$$P = \frac{r(1+r)^m V(0)}{(1+r)^m - 1} = 507.1333.$$

Using the rate $r = 0.085/12 = 0.0071$ we find that the total balance actually being paid is

$$\frac{P}{r}\left(1 - \frac{1}{(1+r)^m}\right) = 51,499.2302 \ .$$

This means that the total fees of bank A equal $1,499.2302$. For bank B the APR per period is $r = 0.092/12 = 0.0077$. The monthly payment is

$$P = \frac{r(1+r)^m V(0)}{(1+r)^m - 1} = 513.0993 \ .$$

Using the rate $r = 0.088/12 = 0.0073$ we find that the total balance actually being paid is

$$\frac{P}{r}\left(1 - \frac{1}{(1+r)^m}\right) = 51,186.8979 \ .$$

This means that the total fees of bank B equal $1,186.8979$. Thus, bank A charges more in fees.

† **14.** Suppose that if you invest in a money market account you can get the annual return of 10% during the next five years. Your trustworthy friend Conman suggest that, instead, you should enter into a business with him, guaranteed to return \$30,000 every year for the next five years, for the initial investment of \$100,000. Assuming you believe him, what is your estimate of the annual worth of the business?

Solution: We have $m = 5$. The interest rate per period is $r = 0.1$. The value of the investment is $V(0) = 100,000$. The annual payment on a loan of this size is

$$P = \frac{r(1+r)^m V(0)}{(1+r)^m - 1} = 26,379.7481 \ .$$

Thus, the annual worth of the business is $30,000 - 26,379.7481 = 3,620.2519$.

† **16.** Using the simple rate convention, find the yield of a 2-year bond traded at par, with face value \$100, paying coupons of \$3.00 every six months.

Solution: The bond has a price of \$100 and pays \$3.00, that is, 3% of its price, every six months. The six-month return is, then, 3%. In order to annualize this rate using the simple interest rate convention we only need to multiply by two, that is, 6%. Since the bond trades at par, the yield is also 6%, as you can verify using expression (2.8) in the book.

† **18.** In the previous problem what should the price P of the one-year pure discount bond be in order to prevent arbitrage opportunities? Explain how to construct arbitrage if the price is instead equal to $\tilde{P} = P + 0.5$.

Solution: One way to solve the previous problem is to construct a portfolio equivalent to a one-year zero-coupon bond with face value \$104.00 by holding the one-year coupon bond and selling short 0.04 units of the six-month zero-coupon bond from that problem at a cost of $102 - 0.04 \cdot 98.20 = 98.072$. This corresponds to the one-year spot rate of 6.0445%, so that the price of the one-year zero-coupon bond with nominal \$100 should be $\frac{100}{1.060445} = 94.30$. If the price of the one-year pure discount bond were 94.80, the bond would be overpriced and we could take advantage of the arbitrage opportunity by selling short one unit of this bond and buying $94.80/98.072 = 0.96664$ units of the portfolio described above. The cost of this is zero. In six-months, the payment and the revenue would match. At maturity, we would have to pay $100 for the one-year pure discount bond and would receive $0.96664 \cdot 104 = 100.53$ from the coupon bond. This is an arbitrage profit.

† 20. In the context of the previous problem you want to lock in the forward rate for the period between the year one and year three. How can you do that by trading in the one-year and the three-year bond?

Solution: We would buy (for example) one unit of the three-year pure discount bond and would sell short $85/96$ units of the one-year pure discount bond. By construction, the net cash flow at the moment the portfolio is set up is zero. In one year we would have to pay $(85/96) \cdot 100 = \$88.542$. Two years later we would receive $100. The annual return of that investment will be the forward rate computed in the previous problem, regardless of the interest rates prevailing in the market at any future time.

3 MODELS OF SECURITIES PRICES IN FINANCIAL MARKETS

† 2. In the single-period model show that equation (3.3) holds.
Solution: After dividing

$$X(1) = \delta_0 B(1) + \delta_1 S_1(1) + \ldots + \delta_N S_N(1)$$

with $1 + r$, we get

$$\bar{X}(1) = \delta_0 + \delta_1 \bar{S}_1(1) + \ldots + \delta_N \bar{S}_N(1) \ .$$

Since

$$X(0) = \delta_0 B(0) + \delta_1 S_1(0) + \ldots + \delta_N S_N(0) \ ,$$

the previous equation can be written as

$$\bar{X}(1) = X(0) + \delta_1 [\bar{S}_1(0) - S_1(0)] + \ldots + \delta_N [\bar{S}_N(1) - S_N(0)] = X(0) + \bar{G} \ .$$

† 4. Show that equation (3.7) holds in the multiperiod model, or at least for the case of two assets and two periods.
Solution: After dividing

$$X(t) = \delta_0(t) B(t) + \delta_1(t) S_1(t) + \ldots + \delta_N(t) S_N(t)$$

with $(1 + r)^t$, we get

$$\bar{X}(t) = \delta_0(t) + \delta_1(t) \bar{S}_1(t) + \ldots + \delta_N(t) S_N(t) \ .$$

Since

$$X(0) = \delta_0(0) B(0) + \delta_1(0) S_1(0) + \ldots + \delta_N(0) S_N(0) \ ,$$

the previous equation can be written as (since $B(0) = 1$)

$$\bar{X}(t) = X(0) + \delta_0(t) - \delta_0(0) + \delta_1(t) \bar{S}_1(0) - \delta_1(0) S_1(0) + \ldots + \delta_N(t) \bar{S}_N(t) - \delta_N(0) S_N(0) \ . \quad (3.1)$$

We have to show that the right-hand side is equal to $X(0) + \bar{G}(t)$. We have

$$\bar{G}(t) = \sum_{s=1}^{t} \delta_1(s) \Delta \bar{S}_1(s) + \ldots + \sum_{s=1}^{t} \delta_N(s) \Delta \bar{S}_N(s) \ .$$

Consider, for example, the terms in the sums corresponding to $s = 1$:

$$\delta_1(1)[\bar{S}_1(1) - S_1(0)] + \ldots + \delta_N(1)[\bar{S}_N(1) - S_N(0)] \ .$$

Using the self-financing condition divided by $(1 + r)^t$, that is,

$$\delta_0(t) + \delta_1(t)\bar{S}_1(t) + \ldots + \delta_N(t)\bar{S}_N(t) = \delta_0(t + 1) + \delta_1(t + 1)\bar{S}_1(t) + \ldots + \delta_N(t + 1)\bar{S}_N(t) \ ,$$

we see that those terms can be written as

$$\delta_0(2) - \delta_0(1) + \delta_1(2)\bar{S}_1(1) - \delta_1(0)S_1(0) + \ldots + \delta_N(2)\bar{S}_N(1) - \delta_N(0)S_N(0) \ . \tag{3.2}$$

Consider now the next terms in $G(t)$ corresponding to $s = 2$:

$$\delta_1(2)[\bar{S}_1(2) - \bar{S}_1(1)] + \ldots + \delta_N(2)[\bar{S}_N(2) - \bar{S}_N(1)] \ .$$

We see that the terms with the negative sign cancel with terms in (3.2). Continuing using the self-financing condition, we see that all the terms in $G(t)$ cancel except

$$[\delta_0(t) - \delta_0(0)] + [\delta_1(t)\bar{S}_1(t) - \delta_1(0)S_1(0)] + \ldots + [\delta_N(t)\bar{S}_N(t) - \delta_N(0)S_1(0)] \ .$$

Comparing with (3.1), we see that we have proved that $\bar{X}(t) = X(0) + \bar{G}(t)$.

† 6. Give an example of a Cox-Ross-Rubinstein model with expected relative stock return equal to 0.1, $E[S(t)/S(t - 1)] = 0.1$, and variance equal to 0.2, $\text{Var}[S(t)/S(t - 1)] = 0.2$. That is, choose the values of parameters p, u, and d so that these conditions are satisfied.

Solution: We have

$$E[S(t)/S(t - 1)] = pu + (1 - p)d, \quad E[(S(t)/S(t - 1))^2] = pu^2 + (1 - p)d^2 \ .$$

Thus, we need to solve the system

$$pu + (1 - p)d = 0.1, \quad pu^2 + (1 - p)d^2 - (pu + (1 - p)d)^2 = 0.2 \ .$$

We get $p = (0.1 - d)/(u - d)$ and

$$d^2(u - 0.1) - d(u^2 - 0.21) + 0.1u^2 - 0.21u = 0 \ .$$

We need to have $0 < p < 1$ and $0 < d < u$. For example, if we take $u = 3$, we get $d = 0.031$ and $p = 0.0232$.

† 10. Continue the previous problem by finding the dynamics of

$$\sin(X), \quad X^4 \cdot Y, \quad \sin(X) \cdot Y \ .$$

Solution:

$$d\sin(X) = \cos(X)dX - \frac{1}{2}\sin(X) \cdot 3^2 dt = [\cos(X)(2 + 5t + X) - 4.5\sin(X)]dt + 3\cos(X)dW_1 \ .$$

We use the previous problem for $d(X^4Y)$:

$$
\begin{aligned}
d(X^4 \cdot Y) &= X^4 dY + Y dX^4 + 12X^3 \cdot 6 \cdot 0.1 dt + 8Y \cdot 12X^3 dt \\
&= [4X^4Y + Y(4X^3(2 + 5t + X) + 54X^2) \\
&\quad + 7.2X^3 + 96YX^3] dt + [8X^4Y + 12YX^3] dW_1 + 6X^4 dW_2 \quad .
\end{aligned}
$$

Finally,

$$
\begin{aligned}
d(\sin(X) \cdot Y) &= \sin(X) dY + Y d\sin(X) + 24 \cos(X) Y dt + 3 \cos(X) \cdot 6 \cdot 0.1 dt \\
&= [4Y \sin(X) + Y(\cos(X)(2 + 5t + X) - 4.5 \sin(X)) + 24Y \cos(X) \\
&\quad + 1.8 \cos(X)] dt + [8Y \sin(X) + 3Y \cos(X)] dW_1 + 6 \sin(X) dW_2 \quad .
\end{aligned}
$$

† **12.** Show that the process $M(t) := W^2(t) - t$ is a martingale, that is, that $E[M(t)|M(s)] = M(s)$ for $s \leq t$.

Solution: One way to show this is to use Itô's rule:

$$dW^2 = 2W dW + dt$$

from which we see that

$$W^2(t) - t = 2 \int_0^t W(s) dW(s) \quad .$$

The right-hand side is a martingale, and we are done. Another way is to write

$$W^2(t) - W^2(s) = (W(t) - W(s))^2 + 2W(s)(W(t) - W(s) \quad .$$

Taking conditional expectation with respect to the information up to time s, and recalling that $W(t) - W(s)$ is independent of that information and of $W(s)$, and that the variance of $W(t) - W(s)$ is $t - s$, we get

$$E_s[W^2(t) - W^2(s)] = t - s \quad ,$$

or

$$E_s[W^2(t) - t] = W^2(s) - s \quad ,$$

which is the martingale property.

† **16.** In the Merton-Black-Scholes model, find $\mathrm{Var}[S^2(t)]$.

Solution: From the book we know that

$$E\left[e^{-\alpha^2/2t + \alpha W(t)}\right] = 1 \quad ,$$

which we use below. Since

$$S^2(t) = e^{(2\mu + \sigma^2)t - 2\sigma^2 t + 2\sigma W(t)}$$

we have (with $\alpha = 2\sigma$)

$$E[S^2(t)] = e^{(2\mu + \sigma^2)t} \ ,$$

and since

$$S^4(t) = e^{(4\mu + 6\sigma^2)t - 8\sigma^2 t + 4\sigma W(t)}$$

we have (with $\alpha = 4\sigma$)

$$E[S^4(t)] = e^{(4\mu + 6\sigma^2)t} \ .$$

From this we can compute the variance as

$$\text{Var}[S(t)] = E[S^4(t)] - (E[S^2(t)])^2 = e^{(4\mu + 2\sigma^2)t}(e^{4\sigma^2 t} - 1) \ .$$

† **22.** Suppose that in a single-period model the stock value at time 1 is not random, but known already at the beginning of the period. Suppose also that the interest rate r is fixed. Find the conditions on $S(0)$, r and $S(1)$ under which there are no arbitrage opportunities in this market.

 Solution: We need to have

$$S(1) = S(0)(1 + r) \ .$$

If $S(1) > S(0)(1 + r)$, we could borrow $S(0)$ and buy the stock. At the end we would have $S(1)$, and would have to return $S(0)(1 + r) < S(1)$, which means we made arbitrage money. Similarly, if $S(1) < S(0)(1 + r)$, we could sell the stock short, and invest $S(0)$ in the bank.

† **24.** Argue that the single-period Arrow-Debreu market is complete if all Arrow-Debreu securities are traded.

 Solution: Let an arbitrary contingent claim be given as

$$C = (c_1, \ldots, c_K)$$

where c_i is the amount to be received or paid (if negative) by the holder at time $t = 1$. This claim can be replicated by buying (selling short if negative) c_i units of Arrow-Debreu security which pays 1 in state i and zero otherwise, and we do this for all $i = 1, \ldots, K$.

† **26.** Consider a single-period CRR model with interest rate 0.05, $S(0) = 10$, $u = 1.2$ and $d = 0.98$. Suppose you have written an option that pays the value of the square root of the absolute value of the difference between the stock price at maturity and \$10.00; that is, it pays $\sqrt{|S(1) - 10|}$. How many shares of the stock should you buy to replicate this payoff? What is the cost of the replicating portfolio?

 Solution: We need to have

$$1.05\delta_0 + 12\delta_1 = \sqrt{|12 - 10|} = 1.4142 \ ,$$

$$1.05\delta_0 + 9.8\delta_1 = \sqrt{|9.8 - 10|} = 0.4472 \ .$$

Solving this system we get

$$\delta_0 = -3.6765, \quad \delta_1 = 0.4395 \quad .$$

Thus, we need to buy 0.4395 shares and the cost of the replicating portfolio is

$$\delta_0 + 10\delta_1 = 0.7189 \quad .$$

4   OPTIMAL CONSUMPTION/PORTFOLIO STRATEGIES

† 2. You have a choice between two investment opportunities. One pays $20,000 with certainty, while the other pays $30,000 with probability 0.2, $6,000 with probability 0.4, and $1,000 with probability 0.4. Your utility is of the type $U(x) = x^\gamma$, $0 < \gamma < 1$. Moreover, you decide that you are indifferent between the choice of receiving $1,000 for sure, or $1,728 and $512 with a fifty-fifty chance. Find your γ, and decide which opportunity you like better.

Solution: We first find γ. We have

$$1,000^\gamma = 0.5 \cdot 1,728^\gamma + 0.5 \cdot 512^\gamma$$

We solve for γ and find that $\gamma = 1/3$. Now we evaluate the utility for each of the two investment opportunities,

$$20,000^{1/3} = 27.1442$$

and

$$0.2 \cdot 30,000^{1/3} + 0.4 \cdot 6,000^{1/3} + 0.4 \cdot 1,000^{1/3} = 17.483$$

Therefore, certain 20,000 is preferred.

† 4. Let $A(x)$ denote the absolute risk aversion of utility function $U(x)$. What is the absolute risk aversion of utility function $V(x) = a + bU(x)$?

Solution: Remember the definition of absolute risk aversion, $A(x) = -\frac{V''(x)}{V'(x)}$. In this case, we have

$$V'(x) = bU'(x), \quad V''(x) = bU''(x)$$

Therefore,

$$-\frac{V''(x)}{V'(x)} = -\frac{U''(x)}{U'(x)} = A(x)$$

† 6. Suppose your utility function is $U(x) = \log(x)$. You are considering leasing a machine that would produce an annual profit of $10,000 with probability $p = 0.4$ or a profit of $8,000 with probability $p = 0.6$. What is the certainty equivalent for this random return?

Solution: The utility of leasing the machine is

$$0.4 \cdot \log(10,000) + 0.6 \cdot \log(8,000) = 9.0765$$

We now look for the constant number C such that

$$U(C) = \log(C) = 9.0765$$

The solution is $C = 8,746.8966$.

15

† 8. Consider a single-period binomial model: The price of the stock at time 0 is $S(0) = 100$. At time 1 it can move up to 110 with probability 1/3, and down to 90 with probability 2/3. There is also a bank account that pays interest $r = 5\%$ per period. The agent has exponential utility $U(X(1)) = -e^{-0.03X(1)}$. If the agent has \$100 as initial capital, how much should she invest in the stock, in order to maximize her expected utility?

Solution: Suppose that the investor invests π dollars in the stock and, therefore, keeps $100 - \pi$ in the bank account. After one period, for each dollar invested in the stock the investor will receive \$1.1 or \$0.9, depending on the outcome. The utility of the investor after one period will be

$$U(\pi) = \frac{1}{3}\left(-e^{-0.03(1.1\pi+1.05(100-\pi))}\right) + \frac{2}{3}\left(-e^{-0.03(0.9\pi+1.05(100-\pi))}\right)$$

We take the derivative with respect to π and make it equal to zero, to get

$$\frac{1}{3}[0.03(1.1-1.05)]\left(-e^{-0.03(1.1\pi+1.05(100-\pi))}\right) + \frac{2}{3}[0.03(0.9-1.05]\left(-e^{-0.03(0.9\pi+1.05(100-\pi))}\right) = 0$$

Multiplying by 3 and rearranging, we get

$$0.0015\left(-e^{-0.03(1.1\pi+1.05(100-\pi))}\right) = (-0.0018)e^{-0.03(0.9\pi+1.05(100-\pi))}$$

and

$$1.2 = e^{0.006\pi}$$

with solution $\pi = 30.3869$. The remainder should be invested in the bond.

† 10. In the context of Example 4.6, use dynamic programming to compute the optimal portfolio for the general power utility, $U(x) = x^\gamma/\gamma$.

Solution: We start the backward algorithm by setting $V(T, x) = x^\gamma/\gamma$. We want to find $V(T-1, x)$. Introduce the notation

$$\tilde{u} = u - (1+r), \quad \tilde{d} = d - (1+r) \ . \tag{4.1}$$

Suppose that the current wealth at time $T - 1$ is $X(T-1) = x$ and the current stock price is $S(T-1) = s$. By the principle of dynamic programming, we have

$$
\begin{aligned}
\gamma V(T-1, x) &= \max_\delta E_{T-1,x}[X^\gamma(T)] \\
&= \max_\delta E_{T-1,x}[\{\delta S(T) + (x - \delta s)(1+r)\}^\gamma] \tag{4.2} \\
&= \max_\delta [p\{\delta s(u - (1+r)) + x(1+r)\}^\gamma \\
&\quad + q\{\delta s(d - (1+r)) + x(1+r)\}^\gamma] \ .
\end{aligned}
$$

We don't have to worry about the budget constraint, already accounted for in (4.2). Differentiating with respect to δ and setting the derivative equal to zero, we get

$$ps\tilde{u}\{\delta s\tilde{u} + x(1+r)\}^{\gamma-1} = -qs\tilde{d}\{\delta s\tilde{d} + x(1+r)\}^{\gamma-1} \ .$$

We now set both sides to the power $\alpha = \frac{1}{\gamma-1}$ and solve for the optimal number of shares $\hat{\delta}$ at time $T-1$ and the optimal proportion $\hat{\Pi}$ to be held in the stock at time $T-1$:

$$\hat{\Pi} := \frac{\hat{\delta}s}{x} = (1+r)\frac{(-q\tilde{d})^\alpha - (p\tilde{u})^\alpha}{\tilde{u}(p\tilde{u})^\alpha - \tilde{d}(-q\tilde{d})^\alpha} \quad . \tag{4.3}$$

We note that optimal proportion $\hat{\Pi}$ at time $T-1$ does not depend on wealth $X(T-1) = x$ nor on the stock price value $S(T-1) = s$ at time $T-1$, but only on model parameters. Substituting the optimal $\hat{\delta} \cdot s = x\hat{\Pi}$ back into (4.2), we see that we get

$$\gamma V(T-1, x) = p\left\{x[\hat{\Pi}\tilde{u} + (1+r)]\right\}^\gamma + q\left\{x[\hat{\Pi}\tilde{d} + (1+r)]\right\}^\gamma = cx^\gamma$$

for some constant c that depends on model parameters only. The next step would be to find $V(T-2, x)$ as (with $S(T-2) = s$)

$$\gamma V(T-2, x) = \max_\delta E_{T-2,x}\left[c\left\{\delta S(T-1) + (x - \delta s)(1+r)\right\}^\gamma\right] \quad .$$

We see that this is of the same form as in (4.2), and thus, the optimization will give the same result for the optimal proportion $\hat{\Pi}$ as before. Therefore, we can show by induction that the optimal proportion $\hat{\Pi}$ does not change with time, and it is always equal to the expression given by (4.3).

† **14.** Find the optimal portfolio for the exponential utility from terminal wealth in continuous time by solving the HJB PDE.

Solution: Trying the function $V(t, x) = 1 - f(t)e^{-g(t)x}$ as a solution to the PDE

$$V_t - \frac{\theta^2}{2}\frac{(V_x)^2}{V_{xx}} + rxV_x = 0, \quad V(T, x) = 1 - e^{-\alpha x} \quad , \tag{4.4}$$

we get

$$e^{-g(t)x}\left[-f'(t) + f(t)g'(t)x + \frac{1}{2}\theta^2 f(t) + rg(t)f(t)x\right] = 0 \quad .$$

Equivalently,

$$f'(t) - \frac{1}{2}\theta^2 f(t) = 0 , \quad g'(t) + rg(t) = 0 ,$$

with the boundary conditions $f(T) = 1, g(T) = \alpha$. This gives

$$f(t) = e^{\theta^2(T-t)/2}, \quad g(t) = \alpha e^{r(T-t)} \quad .$$

The optimal portfolio is

$$\hat{\pi}(t, x) = -\sigma^{-1}\theta\frac{V_x(t, x)}{V_{xx}(t, x)} = \frac{\theta}{\alpha\sigma}e^{-r(T-t)} \quad . \tag{4.5}$$

† **16.** Using the martingale approach in the single-period binomial model, find the optimal portfolio strategy for maximizing $E[\log(X(1)]$ and $E[X^\gamma(1)/\gamma]$, for $\gamma < 1$.

17

Solution: As explained in the book, we have to replicate $\hat{X}(1) = I(\lambda Z(1))$, for an appropriate value of λ. In particular, we need to have

$$I(\lambda \bar{z}^u) = \hat{\delta} S(0) u + (x - \hat{\delta} S(0))(1 + r)$$

and

$$I(\lambda \bar{z}^d) = \hat{\delta} S(0) d + (x - \hat{\delta} S(0))(1 + r) \ ,$$

where z^u, z^d are given in the book, and $\bar{z}^i = z^i / (1 + r)$. Introduce the notation

$$\tilde{u} = u - (1 + r) \ , \quad \tilde{d} = d - (1 + r) \ .$$

For $U(x) = \log(x)$ we have $I(z) = 1/z$ and solving the above system we get

$$\frac{1}{\lambda} = \frac{x(1 + r)(\tilde{d} - \tilde{u})}{\tilde{d}/\bar{z}^u - \tilde{u}/\bar{z}^d}$$

$$\hat{\delta} S(0) = \frac{1}{\tilde{u}} \left[x(1 + r) - \frac{1}{\lambda \bar{z}^u} \right] \ .$$

For $U(x) = x^\gamma / \gamma$ we have $I(z) = z^{1/(\gamma - 1)}$ and solving the above system we get

$$\lambda^{\frac{1}{\gamma - 1}} = \frac{x(1 + r)(\tilde{d} - \tilde{u})}{\tilde{d}(\bar{z}^u)^{\frac{1}{\gamma - 1}} - \tilde{u}(\bar{z}^d)^{\frac{1}{\gamma - 1}}}$$

$$\hat{\delta} S(0) = \frac{1}{\tilde{u}} \left[x(1 + r) - (\lambda \bar{z}^u)^{\frac{1}{\gamma - 1}} \right] \ .$$

† 20. Using the martingale approach in the two-period binomial model, find the optimal portfolio strategy for maximizing $E[1 - \exp\{-\alpha X(1)\}]$.

Solution: Introduce the notation

$$\tilde{u} = u - (1 + r) \ , \quad \tilde{d} = d - (1 + r) \ .$$

As explained in the book, we have to replicate $\hat{X}(2) = I(\lambda \bar{Z}(2))$, for an appropriate value of λ. Let us use the subscript u for the values corresponding to the case when the stock goes up in the first period, and we use the subscript d for the values corresponding to the case when the stock goes down in the first period. The replication in the second period if the stock went up in the first period is done by solving

$$\delta_u(1) S(0) u \tilde{u} + X_u(1)(1 + r) = I(\lambda (z^u)^2 / (1 + r)^2)$$

$$\delta_u(1) S(0) u \tilde{d} + X_u(1)(1 + r) = I(\lambda z^u z^d / (1 + r)^2) \ .$$

We solve these two equations for the wealth $X_u(1)$ after the first period and the number $\delta_u(1)$ of shares in stock to be held in the second period, if the stock went up in the first period. Similarly, we solve for $X_d(1), \delta_d(1)$ the system

$$\delta_d(1) S(0) d \tilde{u} + X_d(1)(1 + r) = I(\lambda z^u z^d / (1 + r)^2)$$

$$\delta_d(1)S(0)d\tilde{d} + X_d(1)(1+r) = I(\lambda(z^d)^2/(1+r)^2) \ .$$

Finally, we solve the system

$$\delta(0)S(0)\tilde{u} + x(1+r) = X_u(1)$$

$$\delta(0)S(0)\tilde{d} + x(1+r) = X_d(1)$$

for the number $\delta(0)$ of shares to be held in the first period, and for λ (here, $X_u(1), X_d(1)$ depend on λ). Alternatively, we could have found λ first, from the condition $E[\bar{Z}(2)X(2)] = x$, which, in our case, is equivalent to

$$x(1+r)^2 = p^2(z^u)^2 I\left(\frac{\lambda(z^u)^2}{(1+r)^2}\right) + 2p(1-p)z^u z^d I\left(\frac{\lambda z^u z^d}{(1+r)^2}\right) + (1-p)^2(z^d)^2 I\left(\frac{\lambda(z^d)^2}{(1+r)^2}\right) \ .$$

†* 22. In the context of Example 4.10, find the optimal portfolio for the exponential utility using the duality approach.

Solution: For $U(x) = 1 - e^{-\alpha x}$ we have

$$U'(x) = \alpha e^{-\alpha x}, \quad I(z) = (U')^{-1}(z) = -\frac{1}{\alpha}\log\left(\frac{z}{\alpha}\right) \ .$$

The optimal wealth level is then

$$\hat{X}(T) = -\frac{1}{\alpha}\log\left(\frac{\hat{\lambda}\bar{Z}(T)}{\alpha}\right) \ .$$

We also know that $\bar{Z}X^{x,\hat{\pi}}$ is a martingale. Then, we can compute

$$\bar{Z}(t)X^{x,\hat{\pi}}(t) = -E_t\left[\frac{\bar{Z}(T)}{\alpha}\log\left(\frac{\hat{\lambda}\bar{Z}(T)}{\alpha}\right)\right] \ .$$

This conditional expectation can be computed directly by using the formula for $Z(T)$ and integrating against the normal density. However, it is somewhat easier to use a Girsanov change of probability and Bayes rule. That is, the above right-hand side is equal to

$$-\frac{e^{-rT}}{\alpha}Z(t)E_t^*\left[\log\left(\frac{\hat{\lambda}\bar{Z}(T)}{\alpha}\right)\right] \ ,$$

where E_t^* is the conditional expectation corresponding to the probability P^*, under which

$$W^*(t) = W(t) + \theta t$$

is a Brownian motion. Using this, the fact that

$$\log(Z(T)) = \theta^2 T/2 - \theta W^*(T)$$

19

and the fact that $E_t^*[W^*(T)] = W^*(t) = W(t) + \theta t$, we get

$$\bar{Z}(t)X^{x,\hat{\pi}}(t) = -\frac{e^{-rT}}{\alpha}Z(t)\left(\log(z/\alpha) - rT + \theta^2 T/2 - \theta^2 t - \theta W(t)\right) \quad .$$

From this we get

$$d\bar{X}(t) = [\ldots]dt + \frac{e^{-rT}}{\alpha}\theta dW(t) \quad .$$

On the other hand, we have

$$d\bar{X}(t) = [\ldots]dt + \bar{\pi}(t)\sigma dW(t) \quad .$$

Comparing the two equations, we get

$$\hat{\pi}(t) = \frac{\theta}{\sigma\alpha}e^{-r(T-t)} \quad .$$

†* **24.** Find the optimal portfolio and consumption strategies for the log utility in continuous-time, by solving the HJB PDE (4.43). (**Hint:** try to find a solution of the HJB PDE of the form $V(t,x) = f(t) + g(t)\log x$.)

Solution: Maximizing the term $U_2(c) - cV_x$ in HJB PDE (4.43) in the book, we get

$$\hat{c}(t,x) = I_2(V_x(t,x)) \quad ,$$

where I_2 is the inverse function of U_2. For $U_2(c) = U_1(c) = \log(x)$ we have $I_2(z) = 1/z$. Thus, the HJB PDE becomes

$$V_t - \frac{\theta^2}{2}\frac{(V_x)^2}{V_{xx}} + rxV_x - \log(V_x) - 1 = 0, \quad V(T,x) = \log(x) \quad . \tag{4.6}$$

Trying the function $V(t,x) = f(t) + g(t)\log x$ as a solution, we get

$$f'(t) + g'(t)\log(x) + \frac{\theta^2}{2}g(t) + rg(t) - \log(g(t)) + \log(x) = 1 \quad .$$

This means that

$$\log(x)[g'(t) + 1] = 0$$

with the boundary condition $g(T) = 1$. Thus,

$$g(t) = T - t + 1 \quad .$$

Then we can also find $f(t)$, but we do not need it. The optimal portfolio is

$$\hat{\pi}(t,x) = -\sigma^{-1}\theta\frac{V_x(t,x)}{V_{xx}(t,x)} = \frac{\theta}{\sigma}x \quad . \tag{4.7}$$

The optimal consumption is

$$\hat{c}(t,x) = \frac{1}{V_x(t,x)} = \frac{x}{T-t+1} \quad . \tag{4.8}$$

†* **28.** Given a random variable C whose value is known by time T, and such that $E[|C|]$ is finite, show that the process $M(t) := E_t[C]$ is a martingale on the time interval $[0, T]$.

Solution: We have

$$E_t[M(s)] = E_t[E_s[C]] = E_s[C] = M(s) \ ,$$

for $s < t$, by properties of conditional expectations (to be found in the last chapter of the book). This is exactly the martingale property.

5 RISK

† 4. Consider a mutual fund F that invests 50% in the risk-free security and 50% in stock A, which has expected return and standard deviation of 10% and 12%, respectively. The risk-free rate is 5%. You borrow the risk-free asset and invest in F so as to get an expected return of 15%. What is the standard deviation of your investment?

Solution: The expected return and standard deviation of the mutual fund F is

$$\mu_F = 0.5 \cdot 0.1 + 0.5 \cdot 0.05 = 0.075 = 7.5\%$$
$$\sigma_F = 0.5 \cdot 0.12 = 0.06 = 6\%$$

We now compute the proportion Π_F of the investment that you will have to put in F and the proportion Π_0 to invest in the risk-free security, in order to achieve the target expected return:

$$0.075\Pi_F + 0.05\Pi_0 = 0.15$$
$$\Pi_F + \Pi_0 = 1$$

with solution $\Pi_F = 4$, $\Pi_0 = -3$ (therefore we are borrowing the risk-free asset). The standard deviation of the investment is

$$\sigma = 4 \cdot 0.06 = 0.24 = 24\%$$

† 10. You can invest in asset 1 with $\mu_1 = 0.1$, $\sigma_1 = 0.3$ and asset 2 with $\mu_2 = 0.2$, $\sigma_2 = 0.5$, with correlation $\rho = 0.2$. You can also invest in the risk-free asset with return $R = 0.05$. Find the optimal mean-variance portfolio for the given mean return $\mu = 0.2$.

Solution: Denote by Π_0, Π_1 the proportions in the risk-free asset, and asset 1, and by $\Pi_2 = 1 - \Pi_0 - \Pi_1$ the proportion in asset 2. We have to have

$$0.05\Pi_0 + 0.1\Pi_1 + 0.2(1 - \Pi_0 - \Pi_1) = 0.2 \ .$$

This gives $\Pi_1 = -1.5\Pi_0$, and thus $\Pi_2 = 1 + 0.5\Pi_0$. Since the risk-free asset has zero variance/covariance, the portfolio variance is given by

$$\sigma^2 = 1.5^2\Pi_0^2 0.3^2 + (1 + 0.5\Pi_0)^2 0.5^2 + 2 \cdot 0.3 \cdot 0.5 \cdot 1.5\Pi_0(1 + 0.5\Pi_0) \ ,$$

or $\sigma^2 = 0.49\Pi_0^2 + 0.7\Pi_0 + 0.25$. Setting the derivative with respect to Π_0 equal to zero, we obtain

$$\Pi_0 = -0.7143, \quad \text{and} \quad \Pi_1 = 1.0714 \ , \quad \Pi_2 = 0.6429 \ .$$

† 12. Suppose that the risk-free rate is 5%. There are three risky portfolios A, B and C with expected returns 15%, 20%, and 25%, respectively, and standard deviations 5%, 10%, and 14%. You can invest in the risk-free security and only one of the risky portfolios. Which one of them would you choose? What if the risk-free rate is 10%?

Solution: The portfolios formed by the risk-free security and one of the risky portfolios will plot in a straight line. For risk-averse investors we want the slope of the straight line as high as possible. The formula for the slope s_i of each of the three possible portfolios is

$$s_i = \frac{\mu_i - R}{\sigma_i}$$

and for a rate of 5% we get, $s_A = 2$, $s_B = 1.5$, $s_C = 1.43$. Therefore we should select portfolio A. When the risk-free rate goes up to 10%, the slopes change to $s_A = 1$, $s_B = 1$, $s_C = 1.07$, and now the optimal risky security is C.

† 14. Compute the historical daily 90% VaR of a portfolio whose daily losses in the last 10 days were, in millions of dollars (minus sign indicates a profit):

$$1, -0.5, -0.1, 0.7, 0.2, 0.1, -0.2, -0.8, -0.3, 0.5 \ .$$

Solution: If we order the losses by size, we get

$$-0.8, -0.5, -0.3, -0.2, -0.1, 0.1, 0.2, 0.5, 0.7, 1 \ .$$

Since there are ten days, the 90% historical VaR is the largest loss, that is VaR = 1 million, because 90% = 9 of the losses are below one million.

† 16. Compute the daily 99% and 95% VaR of a portfolio whose daily return is normally distributed with a mean of 1% and a standard deviation of 0.5%. The current value of the portfolio is $1 million.

Solution: For 99% we have

$$\text{VaR} = X(0)[2.33\sigma - \mu] = 2.33 \cdot 0.005 - 0.01 = 0.00165$$

million, or 1,650 dollars. For 95% we have, since NORMSINV(0.95) = 1.65,

$$\text{VaR} = X(0)[1.65\sigma - \mu] = 1.65 \cdot 0.005 - 0.01 = -0.00175$$

million. In this latter case, the VaR value is negative, hence represents profit. In other words, there is a 5% chance that the daily profit will be less than 1,750 dollars.

† 18. Small investor Taf has 70% of his portfolio invested in a major market-index fund, and 30% in a small-stocks fund. The mean monthly return rate of the market-index fund is 1.5%, with standard deviation 0.9%. The small-stocks fund has the mean monthly return rate of 2.2% with standard deviation of 1.2%. The correlation between the two funds is 0.13.

Assume normal distribution for the return rates. What is the monthly VaR at 99% level for the Taf's portfolio if the portfolio value today is $100,000$?

Solution: The mean return of the portfolio is

$$\mu = 0.7 \cdot 0.015 + 0.3 \cdot 0.022 = 0.0171 \quad .$$

The variance is

$$\sigma^2 = 0.7^2 \cdot 0.009^2 + 0.3^2 \cdot 0.012^2 + 2 \cdot 0.7 \cdot 0.3 \cdot 0.13 \cdot 0.009 \cdot 0.012 = 0.0000585468 \quad .$$

Thus, $\sigma = \sqrt{\sigma^2} = 0.0077$. We have

$$\text{VaR} = X(0)[2.33\sigma - \mu] = 100,000[2.33 \cdot 0.0077 - 0.0171] = 84.1$$

dollars.

6   ARBITRAGE AND RISK-NEUTRAL PRICING

† **2.** Provide detailed no-arbitrage arguments for expression (6.5).

Solution: Suppose that (6.3) does not hold, that is,

$$p(t) + S(t) < Ke^{-r(T-t)} \quad .$$

Then we borrow $Ke^{-r(T-t)}$ from the bank, buy the put and the stock from the borrowed money and still have some extra money left. At maturity, we owe K to the bank. If $K > S(T)$, we exercise the option: we give the stock in return for K dollars, which covers our debt to the bank. We still have that extra money. If $K \leq S(T)$, we sell the stock and have enough to cover the bank debt, and also have that extra money. This is arbitrage.

† **4.** Assume that the future dividends on a given stock S are known, and denote their discounted value at the present time t by $\bar{D}(t)$. Argue the following:

$$c(t) \geq S(t) - \bar{D}(t) - Ke^{-r(T-t)}, \quad p(t) \geq \bar{D}(t) + Ke^{-r(T-t)} - S(t) \quad .$$

Solution: Suppose that the first inequality does not hold, that is,

$$c(t) + \bar{D}(t) + Ke^{-r(T-t)} < S(t) \quad .$$

Then we sell the stock short, use that money to buy the call and deposit $\bar{D}(t) + Ke^{-r(T-t)}$ into the bank, and still have some extra money left. Since we are short the stock, we have to pay the dividends, but that will be covered by using $\bar{D}(t)$ and the interest on it received from the bank. At maturity, we owe $S(T)$, being short the stock and we have K in the bank. If $S(T) > K$, we exercise the call option: we get the stock in return for K dollars from the bank, which covers our short position. We still have that extra money. If $K \geq S(T)$, we use part of K dollars to buy the stock and cover the short position. We still have that extra money. This is arbitrage.

Suppose that the second inequality does not hold, that is,

$$p(t) + S(t) < \bar{D}(t) + Ke^{-r(T-t)} \quad .$$

Then we borrow $\bar{D}(t) + Ke^{-r(T-t)}$ from the bank, use that money to buy the stock and the put option, and still have some extra money left. Since we hold the stock, we receive the dividends, and that will cover our debt of $\bar{D}(t)$ and interest on it to the bank. At maturity, we owe K to the bank. If $S(T) < K$, we exercise the put option: we sell the stock for K dollars, and cover our bank debt. We still have that extra money from the beginning. If $K \leq S(T)$, we sell the stock and cover our bank debt. We still have that extra money. This is arbitrage.

† 6. Why is an American option always worth more than its intrinsic value? (As an example, recall that the intrinsic value at time t for the call option is $\max(S(t) - K, 0)$.)

Solution: Because we can always exercise immediately, and receive the intrinsic value. We have an option of not doing that and waiting, which only increases the option value. More precisely, suppose that the option is worth x, which is less than the intrinsic value y. Than we could borrow x, buy the option, exercise it right away, received y, return x to the bank, and still have $y - x > 0$. This is arbitrage.

† 8. A given stock trades at \$95, and the European calls and puts on the stock with strike price 100 and maturity three months are trading at \$1.97 and \$6 respectively. In one month the stock will pay a dividend of \$1. The prices of one-month and three-month T-bills are \$99.60 and \$98.60, respectively. Construct an arbitrage strategy, if possible.

Solution: We use the put-call parity of Problem 5 (with a single-period discounting):

$$c(t) + \bar{D}(t) + \frac{K}{1+r} = p(t) + S(t)$$

The value of the right-hand side is $6 + 95 = 101$, and the left-hand side yields $1.97 + 100\frac{98.6}{100} + 1\frac{99.50}{100} = 101.566$. The right-hand side is undervalued and the left-hand side is overvalued. We buy the former and sell the latter. That is, we buy the put and the stock and write the call, borrow the present value of the strike price and the present value of the dividend. When the dividend is paid, we use it to cover the loan that the present value of the dividend represents. At maturity of the option, the assets and liabilities match as in the standard put-call parity.

† 10. Consider two European call options on the same underlying and with the same maturity, but with different strike prices, K_1 and K_2 respectively. Suppose that $K_1 > K_2$. Prove that the option prices $c(K_i)$ satisfy

$$K_1 - K_2 > c(K_1) - c(K_2).$$

Solution: This is equivalent to proving that

$$c(K_1) - c(K_2) - K_1 + K_2 < 0$$

We set up a portfolio that results in a cash-flow corresponding to the left-hand side of this expression. That is, we write a call with strike price K_1, buy a call with strike price K_2, lend K_1 and borrow K_2. We denote by r the interest rate between now and maturity of the options. We check all the outcomes at maturity in the following table:

	t=0	At maturity		
		$S \le K_2$	$K_2 < S \le K_1$	$K_1 < S$
Write $c(K_1)$	$c(K_1)$	0	0	$-(S - K_1)$
Buy $c(K_2)$	$-c(K_2)$	0	$(S - K_2)$	$(S - K_2)$
Lend K_1	$-K_1$	$(1+r)K_1$	$(1+r)K_1$	$(1+r)K_1$
Borrow K_2	K_2	$-(1+r)K_2$	$-(1+r)K_2$	$-(1+r)K_2$
TOTAL	a	b	c	d

We have

$$
\begin{aligned}
b &= (1+r)(K_1 - K_2) > 0 \\
c &= (S - K_2) + (1+r)(K_1 - K_2) > 0 \\
d &= (K_1 - K_2) + (1+r)(K_1 - K_2) > 0
\end{aligned}
$$

Therefore, in all the states the outcome is a strictly positive payoff. Then, it has to be the case that $a < 0$, that is, it will cost money to set up the portfolio, or there will be an arbitrage opportunity.

† **12.** Provide no-arbitrage arguments for equation (6.9).

Solution: Suppose first that

$$
F(t) + \bar{D}(t))e^{r(T-t)} > S(t)e^{r(T-t)} \quad .
$$

Then, we take a short position in the forward contract and buy the stock by borrowing $S(t)$ from the bank. In addition, we borrow $\bar{D}(t)$ and deposit it in the bank. We can cover the latter debt from the dividends we receive on the stock. At time T, in addition to the stock we also have $\bar{D}(t)e^{r(T-t)}$ in the bank. We have to return $S(t)e^{r(T-t)}$ to the bank, and we can do that while even making a positive profit, because we deliver the stock and get in exchange $F(t)$ dollars, with $F(t) + \bar{D}(t))e^{r(T-t)} > S(t)e^{r(T-t)}$. This is arbitrage.

Conversely, suppose now that

$$
F(t) < S(t)e^{r(T-t)} - \bar{D}(t))e^{r(T-t)} \quad .
$$

We then sell the stock short, deposit the proceeds in the bank, and take a long position in the forward contract. In addition, we borrow $\bar{D}(t)$ and deposit it in the bank. The latter deposit can be used to pay the dividends for the time interval $[t, T]$. At time T we have $S(t)e^{r(T-t)} - \bar{D}(t))e^{r(T-t)} > F(t)$ in the bank, so we can buy the stock for $F(t)$, cover the short position, and still have some extra money left. Arbitrage.

† **18.** Argue equation (6.13) for forward contracts.

Solution: Suppose first that

$$
F(t) > S(t)e^{(r+u)(T-t)} \quad .
$$

Then, we take a short position in the forward contract and buy $e^{u(T-t)}$ units of the commodity by borrowing $S(t)e^{u(T-t)}$ from the bank. By time T, our commodity worth adjusted for the storage costs is equal to the value of one unit of commodity, and we have to return $S(t)e^{(r+u)(T-t)}$ to the bank. We can do that while even making a positive profit, because we deliver the unit of commodity and get in exchange $F(t)$ dollars, with $F(t) > S(t)e^{(r+u)(T-t)}$. This is arbitrage.

Conversely, suppose now that

$$F(t) < S(t)e^{(r+u)(T-t)} \quad .$$

We then sell $e^{u(T-t)}$ units of the commodity short, meaning we borrow these from some party and sell it to another party. We assume that the party from whom we borrow will also be paying us the storage costs, that she would have had to pay if holding the commodity. Accounting for these costs we receive, the commodity worth we owe to the lending party at time T is not $e^{u(T-t)}$ units, but only one unit. At time t we deposit the proceeds $S(t)e^{u(T-t)}$ in the bank, and take a long position in the forward contract. We can cover the short position of one unit at time T since we have $S(t)e^{(r+u)(T-t)} > F(t)$ in the bank, so we can buy one share for $F(t)$. And we still have some extra money left. Arbitrage.

† **20.** Consider a single-period binomial model of Example 6.3. Suppose you have written an option that pays the value of the squared difference between the stock price at maturity and \$100.00; that is, it pays $[S(1) - 100]^2$. What is the cost $C(0)$ of the replicating portfolio?. Construct arbitrage strategies in the case that the option price is less than $C(0)$ and in the case that it is larger than $C(0)$. Compute the option price as a risk-neutral expected value.

Solution: We observe that this security pays 1 in each state. Thus, it is a risk-free security and can be replicated by investing only in the risk-free asset. We can check that by solving

$$\delta_0(1 + 0.005) + \delta_1 101 = 1$$
$$\delta_0(1 + 0.005) + \delta_1 99 = 1$$

The solution is $\delta_0 = 0.995025$, $\delta_1 = 0$. The cost of the replicating portfolio is \$0.995025. If the price is above \$0.995025, we sell short the option and deposit \$0.995025 in the bank. We keep the difference. At maturity, we cash \$1 from the bank and pay our debt of \$1 (regardless of the state) in the option contract. If the option sells below \$0.995025, we buy it and borrow \$0.995025. We keep the difference. At maturity, our income matches our liability.

It is trivial to compute the risk-neutral expected value, since the payoff is independent of the states:

$$C(0) = \frac{1}{0.005} = 0.995025$$

†* **22.** Given a random variable C whose value is known by time T, and such that $E[|C|]$ is finite, show that the process $M(t) := E_t[C]$ is a martingale on the time interval $[0, T]$.

Solution: We have

$$E_t[M(s)] = E_t[E_s[C]] = E_s[C] = M(s) \ ,$$

for $s < t$, by properties of conditional expectations (to be found in the last chapter of the book). This is exactly the martingale property.

7 OPTION PRICING

† **2.** In a two-period CRR model with $r = 1\%$ per period, $S(0) = 100$, $u = 1.02$, and $d = 0.98$, consider an option that expires after two periods, and pays the value of the squared stock price, $S^2(t)$, if the stock price $S(t)$ is higher than \$100.00 when the option is exercised. Otherwise (when $S(t)$ is less or equal to 100), the option pays zero. Find the price of the European version of this option.

Solution: After two periods, the stock can take three possible values, $S_{uu}(2) = 104.04$, $S_{ud}(2) = 99.96$, $S_{dd}(2) = 96.04$. The payoff of the option will then be $C_{uu}(2) = 10,824.32$ if the stock goes up in price twice, and zero in the other two possible states. In order to price this derivative, we can use risk-neutral pricing. For that, we need to compute the risk-neutral probability p^* as

$$p^* = \frac{(1+r) - d}{u - d} = \frac{1.01 - 0.98}{1.02 - 0.98} = 0.75$$

The price of the derivative is

$$C(0) = \frac{1}{1.01^2}(0.75^2 \cdot 10,824.32) = 5,968.71$$

where we only needed to take into account the state resulting if the stock goes up twice and the risk-neutral probability of this event, because the other two states have zero payoffs.

† **4.** Consider a single-period binomial model with two periods where the stock has an initial price of \$100 and can go up 15% or down 5% in each period. The price of the European call option on this stock with strike price \$115 and maturity in two periods is \$5.424. What should be the price of the risk-free security that pays \$1 after one period regardless of what happens? We assume, as usual, that the interest rate r per period is constant.

Solution: In order to compute the price of the risk-free security we need the interest rate. It is important to observe that the call option only pays if the stock goes up all five times. In that case, the price of the stock is $100(1.15^2) = 132.25$, and the payoff of the option $132.25 - 115 = 17.25$. If the stock goes down a single time, the option will be out-of-the-money and its payoff will be zero. Therefore, using risk-neutral pricing, for unknown risk-neutral probability p^* and interest rate per period r, we need to have

$$5.424 = \frac{1}{(1+r)^2}(p^*)^2 17.25$$

or, simplifying,

$$1 + r = 1.723 p^*$$

We have two unknowns. We have another equation for the same unknowns from the formula for the risk-neutral probability,

$$p^* = \frac{(1+r) - d}{u - d} = \frac{(1+r) - 0.95}{1.15 - 0.95}$$

The solution to the two equations is $p^* = 0.6$, $r = 0.07$. The price of the risk-free security is

$$\frac{1}{1.07} = 0.9346$$

† **6.** Suppose that the stock price today is $S(t) = 2.00$, the interest rate is $r = 0\%$, and the time to maturity is 3 months. Consider an option whose Black-Scholes price is given by the function

$$V(t, s) = s^2 e^{2(T-t)} \quad,$$

where the time is in annual terms. What is the option price today? What is the volatility of the stock equal to?

Solution: The price is

$$V(t, s) = s^2 e^{2(T-t)} = 4e^0.5 = 6.5949 \quad.$$

The function $V(t, s)$ has to satisfy the Black-Scholes equation. We have $V_t = -2s^2 e^{2(T-t)}$, $V_{ss} = 2e^{2(T-t)}$, which means that

$$V_t + \frac{1}{2} \cdot 2s^2 V_{ss} = 0$$

from which we recognize that $\sigma^2 = 2$, thus $\sigma = \sqrt{2}$.

† **10.** Verify that the Black-Scholes formula for the European put option can be obtained from the formula for the call option using put-call parity. (**Hint:** You can use the fact that $1 - N(x) = N(-x)$ for the normal distribution function.)

Solution: We have

$$p(0) = c(0) + Ke^{-rT} - S(0) = S(0)(N(d_1) - 1) + Ke^{-rT}(1 - N(d_2)) = Ke^{-rT}N(-d_2) - S(0)N(-d_1).$$

† **12.** In order to avoid the problem of implied volatilities being different for different strike prices and maturities, a student of the Black-Scholes theory suggests making the stock's volatility σ a function of K and T, $\sigma(K, T)$. What is wrong with this suggestion, at least from the theoretical/modeling point of view? (In practice, though, traders might use different volatilities for pricing options with different maturities and strike prices.)

Solution: The stock's volatility σ in the Merton-Black-Scholes model is a constant associated with the given stock. Thus, theoretically, it cannot change with the strike price and the maturity of options written on the stock.

† 14. In a two-period CRR model with $r = 1\%$ per period, $S(0) = 100$, $u = 1.02$ and $d = 0.98$, consider an option that expires after two periods, and pays the value of the squared stock price, $S^2(t)$, if the stock price $S(t)$ is higher than \$100.00 when the option is exercised. Otherwise (when $S(t)$ is less or equal to 100), the option pays zero. Find the price of the American version of this option.

Solution: We present the corresponding tree for the stock price.

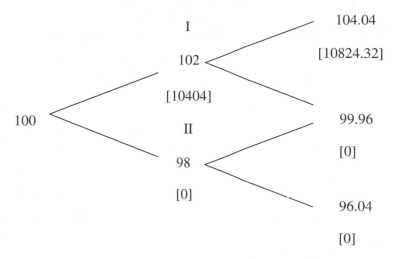

In brackets we record the payoff of the American option if we exercise it in the corresponding node. In node II the payoff and value of un-exercised option is zero. In node I, if we exercise the option, the payoff is $102^2 = 10,404$. We have to compare this payoff with the value of the un-exercised option. For that, we need to compute the risk-neutral probability p^* as

$$p^* = \frac{(1+r) - d}{u - d} = \frac{1.01 - 0.98}{1.02 - 0.98} = 0.75$$

The value of the un-exercised option at that node is

$$\frac{1}{1.01}(0.75 \cdot 10,824.32) = 8,037.86.$$

Therefore, it is optimal to exercise early at this node. We now compute the price of the option at the initial moment as

$$A(0) = \frac{1}{1.01}(0.75 \cdot 10,404) = 7725.743.$$

† 16. Find the price of a 3-month European call option with $K = 100$, $r = 0.05$, $S(0) = 100$, $u = 1.1$ and $d = 0.9$ in the binomial model, if a dividend amount of $D = \$5$ is to be paid at time $\tau = 1.5$ months. Use the binomial tree with time step $\Delta t = 1/12$ years to model the process $S_G(t) = S(t) - e^{-r(\tau - t)}D$ for $t < \tau$.

Solution: As usual, we assume that $r = 0.05$ is the annual interest rate. In the following graph we represent the tree for the stock S and for its value S_G net of dividends, recorded in the brackets:

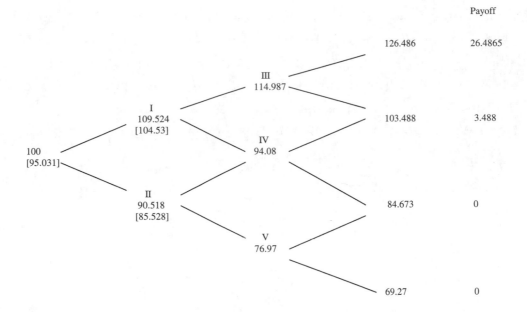

Payoff

The initial price of the stock net of the dividend is $S_G(0) = S(0) - e^{-r\tau}D = 100 - e^{-0.05 \cdot 1.5/12} \cdot 5 = 95.0312$. This part of the price of the stock can go up or down with factors u or d. The total price $S(t)$ of the stock, including dividend, is found from $S(t) = S_G(t) + e^{-0.05(\tau-t)}5$. After the second period the dividend has already been paid and the price of the stock net of the dividend is the total price of the stock, so we keep using u and d to track the possible values of the stock, but do not have to add the dividend.

We now compute the price of the option using backward induction. In node V the price is trivially zero. In nodes III and IV we can use risk-neutral probability, since the dividend has already been paid, or the replicating portfolio method. Since there are dividends, we cannot use the usual risk-neutral probability and we will have to find the replicating portfolio in the previous nodes. Thus, we decide to use this procedure for the whole tree. As usual, we denote δ_0 the investment at the risk-free rate and δ_1 the number of shares to hold. In node III, we have

$$\delta_0 e^{0.05/12} + \delta_1 126.4865 = 26.4865$$
$$\delta_0 e^{0.05/12} + \delta_1 103.4889 = 3.4889$$

with solution $\delta_0 = -99.5842$; $\delta_1 = 1$. The value of the option at node III is, then,

$$C_{III}(2) = 114.9877 - 99.5842 = 15.4035$$

For node IV,

$$\delta_0 e^{0.05/12} + \delta_1 103.4899 = 3.4899$$
$$\delta_0 e^{0.05/12} + \delta_1 84.673 = 0$$

36

with solution $\delta_0 = -15.6349$; $\delta_1 = 0.1854$. The price of the option at node IV is, then,

$$C_{IV}(2) = 0.1854 \cdot 94.081 - 15.6349 = 1.8097$$

Now, we have to take into consideration that between $t = 1$ and $t = 2$ the dividend is paid. An investor that buys one share of stock at moment $t = 1$, at moment $t = 2$ will have one share of the stock plus the future value of the dividend, $5e^{0.05/24}$. Thus, we solve for the replicating portfolio at node I from

$$\begin{aligned}
\delta_0 e^{0.05/12} + \delta_1(114.9877 + 5e^{0.05/24}) &= 15.4305 \\
\delta_0 e^{0.05/12} + \delta_1(94.081 + 5e^{0.05/24}) &= 1.8097
\end{aligned}$$

with solution $\delta_0 = -62.3594$; $\delta_1 = 0.6502$. The price of the option at node I is, then,

$$C_I(1) = 0.6502 \cdot 109.524 - 62.3594 = 8.8534$$

Similarly, in node II we have,

$$\begin{aligned}
\delta_0 e^{0.05/12} + \delta_1(94.081 + 5e^{0.05/24}) &= 1.8097 \\
\delta_0 e^{0.05/12} + \delta_1(76.975 + 5e^{0.05/24}) &= 0
\end{aligned}$$

with solution $\delta_0 = -8.6379$; $\delta_1 = 0.1058$. The price of the option at node II is, then,

$$C_{II}(1) = 0.1058 \cdot 90.518 - 8.6379 = 0.9387$$

Finally, at the initial point we have

$$\begin{aligned}
\delta_0 e^{0.05/12} + \delta_1 109.524 &= 8.8534 \\
\delta_0 e^{0.05/12} + \delta_1 90.518 &= 0.9387
\end{aligned}$$

with solution $\delta_0 = -36.6024$; $\delta_1 = 0.4164$. The price of the option at the initial time is, then,

$$C(0) = 0.4164 \cdot 100 - 36.6024 = 5.0403$$

† **18.** Consider the following two-period setting: the price of a stock is \$50. Interest rate per period is 2%. After one period the price of the stock can go up to \$55 or drop to \$47 and it will pay (in both cases) a dividend of \$3. If it goes up the first period, the second period it can go up to \$57 or down to \$48. If it goes down the first period, the second period it can go up to \$48 or down to \$41. Compute the price of an American put option with strike price $K = 45$ that matures at the end of the second period.

Solution: In the following graph we present the tree corresponding to the stock and put payoff:

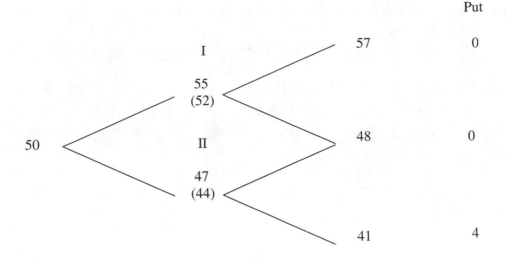

In parenthesis we present the stock prices after dividends are paid. We solve recursively. Obviously, in node I the put is worth 0. In node II, if we exercise the option we get $45 - 44 = 1$ (since we would exercise after the dividend is paid). We compute the value of the un-exercised option and take the higher of the two. In order to compute the value of the un-exercised option we compute the value of the replicating portfolio, by finding the number of shares δ_1 and the amount δ_0 to be deposited in the bank:

$$
\begin{aligned}
1.02\delta_0 + 48\delta_1 &= 0 \\
1.02\delta_0 + 41\delta_1 &= 4
\end{aligned}
$$

with solutions $\delta_1 = -4/7$ and $\delta_0 = 26.89$. The value of the put is, then,

$$
P_I(1) = 26.89 - (4/7)44 = 1.748
$$

This is larger than one, and therefore, we will not exercise the option until maturity. The replicating portfolio at the initial node is obtained from

$$
\begin{aligned}
1.02\delta_0 + 55\delta_1 &= 0 \\
1.02\delta_0 + 47\delta_1 &= 1.748
\end{aligned}
$$

with solutions $\delta_1 = -0.2185$ and $\delta_0 = 11.7812$. The value of the put is, then,

$$
P(0) = 11.7812 - 0.2185 \cdot 50 = 0.8568.
$$

† **20.** Consider a Merton-Black-Scholes model with $r = 0.07$, $\sigma = 0.3$, $T = 0.5$ years, $S(0) = 100$, and a call option with the strike price $K = 100$. Using the normal distribution table (or an appropriate software program), find the price of the call option, when there are no dividends. Repeat this exercise when (a) the dividend rate is 3%; (b) the dividend of $3.00 is paid after three months.

Solution: With no dividends we get

$$d_1 = 0.2711, \quad d_2 = 0.0589, \quad N(d_1) = 0.6068, \quad N(d_2) = 0.5235, \quad C = 10.1338 \; .$$

When the dividend rate is 3% we get

$$d_1 = 0.2003 \;, \quad d_2 = -0.0118, \quad N(d_1) = 0.5794, \quad N(d_2) = 0.4953, \quad C = 9.2506 \; .$$

When the dividend of \$3.00 is paid after three months, we replace $S(0) = 100$ by $S(0) - D(0) = 100 - 3e^{-0.25r} = 97.0524$ and get

$$d_1 = 0.13 \;, \quad d_2 = -0.0821, \quad N(d_1) = 0.5517, \quad N(d_2) = 0.4673, \quad C = 8.4253 \; .$$

† 22. In the context of the previous two problems, with no dividends, compute the price of the chooser option, for which the holder can choose at time $t_1 = 0.25$ years whether to hold the call or the put option.

Solution: For the price of a call option maturing at t_1 we get

$$d_1 = 0.1917, \quad d_2 = 0.0417, \quad N(d_1) = 0.576, \quad N(d_2) = 0.5166, \quad C = 6.8343 \; .$$

For the price of a put option maturing at t_1 and with strike price $Ke^{-r(T-t_1)} = 98.2652$ we get

$$d_1 = 0.3083, \quad d_2 = -0.1583, \quad N(d_1) = 0.6211, \quad N(d_2) = 0.5629, \quad P = 4.3149 \; .$$

The price of the chooser option is $C + P = 11.1492$.

† 24. Provide a proof for expression (7.43) for the price of a digital option. Compute the price if the option pays \$1.00 if the stock price at maturity is larger than \$100.00, and it pays \$0.00 otherwise. Use the same parameters as in the previous three problems.

Solution: The first equality in (7.43) is obvious. The second equality is proved in Appendix 7.9 in the book. The price is $N(0.0589) = 0.5235$.

† 26. Let $S(0) = \$100.00$, $K_1 = \$92.00$, $K_2 = \$125.00$, $r = 5\%$. Find the Black-Scholes formula for the option paying in three months \$10.00 if $S(T) \leq K_1$ or if $S(T) \geq K_2$, and zero otherwise, in the Black-Scholes continuous-time model.

Solution: The price is given by

$$
\begin{aligned}
10e^{-3r/12} E^*[\mathbf{1}_{\{S(T) \leq K_1 \text{ or } S(T) \geq K_2\}}] &= 9.8758(P^*[S(T) \leq K_1] + P^*[S(T) \geq K_2]) \\
&= 9.8758[1 - N(d_2(K_1)) + N(d_2(K_2))] \; .
\end{aligned}
$$

† 30. Show that, if S is modeled by the Merton-Black-Scholes model, then S and its futures price have the same volatility.

Solution: We have

$$dF(t) = e^{r(T-t)}dS(t) - re^{r(T-t)}S(t)dt = F(t)[(\mu - r)dt + \sigma dW(t)]$$

We see that the volatility is the same.

† 32. Compute the price of a European call on the yen. The current exchange rate is 108, the strike price is 110, maturity is three months and t he price of a three-month T-bill is $98.45. We estimate the annual volatility of the yen-dollar exchange rate to be 15%. A three-month pure-discount yen-denominated risk-free bond trades at 993 yen (nominal 1,000).

Solution: We compute the domestic interest rate from the domestic bond:

$$100e^{-0.25r} = 98.45$$

with solution $r = 6.2486\%$. Similarly, we compute the Japanese rate,

$$1000e^{-0.25r_f} = 993$$

with solution $r_f = 2.81\%$. We observe that, in order to apply the Black-Scholes formula, we need the exchange rate expressed in dollars per yen (and not the other way around, as quoted in the problem). We now compute the discounted value of the exchange rate -dollars per yen-,

$$\frac{1}{108}e^{-0.0281 \cdot 0.25} = 0.009194$$

and we can now apply the formula with 0.009194 for the underlying and 1/110 for strike price. We get $C(0) = 0.00041064$, representing the value of the right (in dollars) to buy one yen at an exchange rate of 110 yens per dollar, in three months.

8   FIXED INCOME MARKET MODELS
AND DERIVATIVES

† 2. The price of three-month and nine-month T-bills are \$98.788 and \$96.270, respectively. In our model of the term structure, three months from today the six-month interest rate will be either 5.5% or 5% (in equivalent annual terms). Compute the price of a three-month European put written on the nine-month pure discount bond, with strike price \$97.5.

Solution: We compute the three-month interest rate (in equivalent annual terms) from

$$99.788 = \frac{100}{(1+r)^{1/4}}$$

with solution 5%. We now compute the risk neutral probabilities implicit in our model of interest rates from

$$96.27 = \frac{100}{(1.05)^{1/4}}\left(p\frac{100}{(1.055)^{1/2}} + (1-p)\frac{100}{(1.05)^{1/2}}\right)$$

$$= \frac{100}{(1.05)^{1/4}}(p \cdot 97.358 + (1-p) \cdot 97.59)$$

with solution $p = 0.6$. The price of the put is, then,

$$P(0) = \frac{100}{(1.05)^{1/4}}(p \cdot (97.5 - 97.358) + (1-p) \cdot 0) = 0.0839$$

† 4. In Example 8.3 find the price of the at-the-money call option on the three-year bond, with option maturity equal to two years.

Solution: The price of the three-year bond is

$$\frac{1}{r_3^3} = \frac{1}{1.065^3} = 0.828$$

Two years from now, it will be a one-year bond and will take one of the following three possible values,

$$\frac{1}{1.086} = 0.921; \quad \frac{1}{1.0748} = 0.930; \quad \frac{1}{1.0650} = 0.939$$

The value of the call has to be the present value of the expected payoff under the risk-neutral probability, that is,

$$C(0) = \frac{1}{1.06^2}[0.5^2(0.921 - 0.828) + 2(0.5^2)(0.930 - 0.828) + 0.5^2(0.939 - 0.828)] = 0.091$$

† 10. Show that the interest rate $r(t)$ in the Vasicek model has a normal distribution. (**Hint:** The Vasicek SDE can be solved for an explicit solution. It may help to find the SDE for the process $r(t)e^{at}$.) Show also that this distribution converges for $t \to \infty$.

Solution: For the process $dr = a(b - r)dt + \sigma dW$ we have

$$d(r(t)e^{at}) = e^{at}[abdt + \sigma dW]$$

from which

$$r(t) = e^{-at}\left[r(0) + ab\int_0^t e^{as}ds + \int_0^t e^{as}dW(s)\right]$$

Since $\int_0^t e^{as}ds = (e^{at} - 1)/a$, we get

$$E[r(t)] = e^{-at}r(0) + b(1 - e^{-at})$$

which converges to b as t goes to infinity. Moreover,

$$Var[r(t)] = e^{-2at}\int_0^t e^{2as}ds = \frac{1}{2a}(1 - e^{-2at})$$

which converges to $1/2a$ as t goes to infinity.

† 12. In the previous problem, show that $P(t, T) = \frac{P(0,T)}{P(0,t)}\exp\{(T - t)[f(0, t) - r(t) - \frac{\sigma^2}{2}t(T - t)]\}$.

Solution: Solving the previous problem with $dr(t) = \beta(t)dt + \sigma dW$, you can find that

$$B(t, T) = T - t, \quad A(t, T) = \int_t^T \beta(u)(T - u)du + \frac{\sigma^2}{2}\frac{(T - t)^3}{3}$$

Then, we can write

$$p(t, T) = \frac{P(0, T)}{P(0, t)}e^{A(t,T)-(T-t)r(t)+A(0,t)-tr(0)-A(0,T)+Tr(0)}$$

We also have

$$f(0, t) = -\frac{\partial}{\partial T}A(0, t) + r(0) = -\int_0^t \beta(s)ds + \frac{\sigma^2}{2}(T - t)^2 + r(0)$$

From this we can find an expression for $r(0)$ in terms of $f(0, t)$. Moreover, we can find

$$A(t, T) + A(0, t) - A(0, T) = -(T - t)\int_0^t \beta(s)ds + \frac{\sigma^2}{2}\left[\frac{(T - t)^3}{3} + \frac{t^3 - T^3}{3}\right]$$

Plugging this expression and the expression for $r(0)$ in the above expression for $P(t, T)$, we get the desired representation.

† 14. Let $\sigma(t)$ be a deterministic function such that $\int_0^T \sigma^2(u)du$ is finite. Consider the process

$$Z(t) = e^{\int_0^t \sigma(u)dW(u)-\frac{1}{2}\int_0^t \sigma^2(u)du} \quad .$$

Use Itô's rule to show that this process satisfies

$$dZ = \sigma Z dW \quad .$$

Deduce that this process is a martingale process. Use this fact to find the moment-generating function

$$f(y) = E\left[e^{yX}\right]$$

of the random variable $X = \int_0^T \sigma(u)dW(u)$. Finally, argue that X is normally distributed, with mean zero and variance $\int_0^T \sigma^2(u)du$.

Solution: Using the fact that for $X(t) = \int_0^t \sigma(u)dW(u)$ we have $dX = \sigma dW$, Itô's rule on $Z(t) = e^{X(t) - \frac{1}{2}\int_0^t \sigma^2(u)du}$ gives $dZ = \sigma Z dW$. Thus this is a local martingale. It can be shown that it is actually a martingale. This means that $E[Z(t)] = 1$. We now use this on the process Z_y such that $dZ_y = y\sigma Z_y dW$. We get

$$1 = E[Z_y(T)] = E\left[e^{y\int_0^t \sigma(u)dW(u) - \frac{y^2}{2}\int_0^t \sigma^2(u)du}\right]$$

This gives us

$$E[e^{yX}] = e^{\frac{y^2}{2}\int_0^t \sigma^2(u)du}$$

We recognize this as a moment generating function of a normal distribution with mean zero and variance $\int_0^T \sigma^2(u)du$.

† 16. Do you think that the put-call parity holds in the presence of default risk? Why?

Solution: The put-call parity argument is based on the fact that the payoff of the options is paid at maturity and that holding a call plus discounted K dollars in bank results in the same payoff at maturity as holding a put and a share of the stock. This is not necessarily true in the presence of default risk, since the payoffs may change if there is default before maturity. Thus, the put-call parity does not have to hold.

† 20. You are a party to a swap deal with a notional principal of $100 that has 4 months left to maturity. The payments take place every three months. As a part of the swap deal you have to pay the three-month LIBOR rate, and in exchange you receive the fixed 8% rate (total annually) on the notional principal. The prices of the one-month and four-month risk-free pure discount bonds (nominal $100) are $99.6 and $98.2, respectively. At the last payment date the three-month LIBOR was 7%. Compute the value of the swap.

Solution: We present a more intuitive solution than what we did in the book (where we used equation (8.66)). In order to easier price the swap, we assume that the principal is also exchanged. We first compute the fixed component of the swap. There is a payment of $2 coming in one month, and then a final payment of $102 (since we assumes the principal is included) in four months. The value of this position is

$$F = 2 \times 0.996 + 102 \times 0.982 = 102.156$$

where we use $\frac{1}{1+r} = \frac{P}{100}$. The floating part V has a payment of $\$\frac{7}{4} = 1.75$ coming in one month. We do not know the final payment $100(1 + \delta T L)$, but we know from the definition

43

of the LIBOR rate L in one month that we have $(1 + \Delta TL)P = 100$, where P is the price of the bond (\$100 nominal) in one month. This means that the value of the final payment is going to be \$100 in one month, or $\$100 \cdot 0.996$ today. Therefore, the floating part V has the value

$$V = 1.75 \times 0.996 + 100 \cdot 0.996 = 101.342$$

The value of the swap for the party that pays the floating rate is

$$F - V = 102.156 - 101.342 = 0.813$$

† **22.** Show that the value of the swaption $S^+(T)$ is equal to the value of the cash flow of call options $\Delta T[R(T) - \tilde{R}]^+$ paid at times $t = T_1, \ldots, T_n$, where $R(T)$ is the swap rate at time T, for the swap starting at $t = T$ and maturing at $t = T_n$. (**Hint:** Use the principle for pricing interest-rate derivatives, properties of conditional expectations, and expression (8.68) in order to show that the value of this cash flow is equal to the value of $S^+(T)$.)

Solution: The time-t value of the swaption is

$$E_t\left[e^{-\int_t^T r(s)ds} \left\{ E_T\left[\sum_{j=1}^n e^{-\int_T^{T_j} r(s)ds} \Delta T (L(T_{j-1}, T_j) - \tilde{R}) \right] \right\}^+ \right]$$

$$= E_t\left[e^{-\int_t^T r(s)ds} \left\{ E_T\left[\sum_{j=1}^n e^{-\int_T^{T_j} r(s)ds} \left(\frac{1}{P(T_{j-1}, T_j)} - 1 - \Delta T\tilde{R} \right) \right] \right\}^+ \right]$$

$$= E_t\left[e^{-\int_t^T r(s)ds} \left\{ E_T\left[\left(\sum_{j=1}^n e^{-\int_T^{T_{j-1}} r(s)ds} E_{T_{j-1}}\left[e^{-\int_{T_{j-1}}^T r(s)ds} \right] \frac{1}{P(T_{j-1}, T_j)} \right. \right. \right. \right.$$
$$\left. \left. \left. \left. - \sum_{j=1}^n e^{-\int_T^{T_j} r(s)ds} (1 + \Delta T\tilde{R}) \right) \right] \right\}^+ \right]$$

$$= E_t\left[e^{-\int_t^T r(s)ds} \left\{ E_T\left[\left(\sum_{j=1}^n e^{-\int_T^{T_{j-1}} r(s)ds} - P(T, T_j)(1 + \Delta T\tilde{R}) \right) \right] \right\}^+ \right]$$

$$= E_t\left[e^{-\int_t^T r(s)ds} \left\{ E_T\left[\left(1 - P(T, T_n) - \Delta T\tilde{R} \sum_{j=1}^n P(T, T_j) \right) \right] \right\}^+ \right]$$

$$= E_t\left[e^{-\int_t^T r(s)ds} [R(T) - \tilde{R}]^+ \Delta T \sum_{j=1}^n P(T, T_j) \right]$$

$$= E_t\left[e^{-\int_t^T r(s)ds} [R(T) - \tilde{R}]^+ \Delta T E_T\left[\sum_{j=1}^n e^{-\int_T^{T_j} r(s)ds} \right] \right]$$

$$= E_t\left[\sum_{j=1}^n e^{-\int_t^{T_j} r(s)ds} [R(T) - \tilde{R}]^+ \Delta T \right] ,$$

which is the value of the cash flows at time t.

† 24. Consider a **floating-rate coupon bond** which pays a coupon c_i at time T_i, $i = 1, \ldots, n$, where the coupons are given by

$$c_i = (T_i - T_{i-1})L(T_{i-1}, T_i)$$

and $T_i - T_{i-1} = \Delta T$ is constant. Show that the value of this bond at time $t < T_0$ is equal to $P(t, T_0)$.

Solution: Denote $P = P(T_{i-1}, T_i)$. The price of c_i is equal to

$$
\begin{aligned}
E_t \left[e^{-\int_t^{T_i} r(s)ds} \frac{1 - P}{P} \right] &= E_t \left[E_{T_{i-1}} \left[e^{-\int_{T_{i-1}}^{T} r(s)ds} \right] e^{-\int_t^{T_{i-1}} r(s)ds} \frac{1 - P}{P} \right] \\
&= E_t \left[e^{-\int_t^{T_{i-1}} r(s)ds} (1 - P) \right] = p(t, T_{i-1}) - p(t, T_i)
\end{aligned}
$$

If the floating rate coupon bond pays 1 dollar at maturity T_n, the price of which today is $p(t, T_n)$, then the total value of the bond is

$$p(t, T_n) + \sum_{i=1}^{n} [p(t, T_{i-1}) - P(t, T_i)] = p(t, T_0) \quad .$$

9 HEDGING

† 2. Show that the payoff given by equation (9.6) is, indeed, equal to the payoff of the butterfly spread. Also show that the butterfly spread can be created by buying a put option with a low strike price, buying another put option with a high strike price, and selling two put options with the strike price in the middle.

Solution: The case $K_2 \leq S(T) \leq K_3$ is done in the book.

$$\text{If } S(T) \leq K_1, \text{ then } C = 0 + 0 - 0 = 0$$

$$\text{If } K_1 \leq S(T) \leq K_2, \text{ then } C = S(T) - K_1 + 0 - 0 = S(T) - K_1$$

$$\text{If } S(T) \geq K_3, \text{ then } C = S(T) - K_1 + S(T) - K_3 - 2S(T) + 2K_2 = 2K_2 - (K_1 + K_3) = 0$$

† 4. The stock of the pharmaceutical company "Pills Galore" is trading at $103. The European calls and puts with strike price $100 and maturity in one month trade at $5.60 and $2.20, respectively. In the next three weeks the FDA will announce its decision about an important new drug the company would like to commercialize. You estimate that if the decision is positive the stock will jump to above $110, and if the decision is negative it will drop below $95. Is it possible to construct a strategy that will yield a profit if your estimates are correct? Explain.

Solution: Let us assume $r = 0$ for simplicity. One way of solving the problem is to construct a portfolio of calls and puts that would make money if $S > 110$ and if $S < 95$. We can buy n_C calls and n_P puts for a total value V of

$$V = n_C 5.6 + n_P 2.2$$

Let us set the strike price of both calls and puts at 100. We try to find a number of calls and puts that will allow us to break even at the boundaries 110 and 95:

$$(110 - 100)n_C = V$$
$$(100 - 95)n_P = V$$

This gives $2n_C = n_P$. We now check that a portfolio formed by n calls and $2n$ puts does the job:

$$\text{if } S < 100 : \text{ then } 2n(100 - S) - 10n = 2n(95 - S)$$
$$\text{if } S \geq 100 : \text{ then } n(S - 100) - 10n = n(S - 110)$$

We see that the profit is positive if our estimates are correct.

† 6. Consider a two-period binomial model with a stock that trades at $100. Each period the stock can go up 25% or down 20%. The interest rate is 10%. Your portfolio consists of one share of the stock. You want to trade so that the value of your modified portfolio will not drop below $90 at the end of the second period. Describe the steps to be taken in order to achieve this goal. Only the stock and the bank account are available for trading.

Solution: We represent the tree in the following graph:

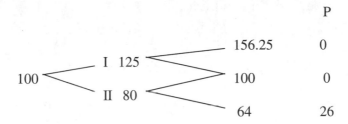

If we don't want to invest extra money, one way of accomplishing the hedge is simply to sell the stock share and deposit the money in the bank. Another standard way of hedging the risk of a drop in a stock price is to replicate a position equivalent to holding a put option and the stock. For this we need to invest extra cash in the portfolio. We describe the latter hedge. We set the strike price at $K = 90$, because that is the lowest amount we want to have. At node I the value of the put option is zero and the replication conditions for the put are

$$\delta_1 156.25 + \delta_0 1.1 = 0$$
$$\delta_1 100 + \delta_0 1.1 = 0$$

with the solution $\delta_1 = 0$, $\delta_0 = 0$, and the cost of 0. At node II, the replication conditions are

$$\delta_1 100 + \delta_0 1.1 = 0$$
$$\delta_1 64 + \delta_0 1.1 = 26$$

with the solution $\delta_1 = -0.722$, $\delta_0 = 65.64$ for a cost of the option at node II of $65.64 - 0.722 \cdot 80 = 7.88$. At the initial node the replication conditions are

$$\delta_1 125 + \delta_0 1.1 = 0$$
$$\delta_1 80 + \delta_0 1.1 = 7.88$$

with the solution $\delta_1 = -0.175$, $\delta_0 = 19.89$, for a cost of the option at the initial node of $19.89 - 0.175 \cdot 100 = 2.39$. This is the extra money we need.

The strategy is, then, as follows. We have one share in our portfolio and we sell 0.175 shares and deposit in the bank $0.175 \cdot 100 + 2.39 = 19.89$. After one period, we will have in the bank $19.89 \cdot 1.1 = 21.88$. If the stock is at node I, we will have to buy back 0.175 shares, for a value of $0.175 \cdot 125 = 21.88$. In the next period, the total value of the portfolio will be 156.25 or 100. If the stock is at node II, we will have to keep $1 - 0.722 = 0.278$ shares. We will sell $0.825 - 0.278 = 0.547$ shares for a total of $0.547 \cdot 80 = 43.76$. We will have in the bank $43.76 + 19.89 \cdot 1.1 = 65.64$. In the next period, if the stock goes up, the value of the portfolio will be $0.278 \cdot 100 + 65.64 \cdot 1.1 = 100$. If the stock goes down, the value of the portfolio will be $0.278 \cdot 64 + 65.64 \cdot 1.1 = 90$.

† **10.** Consider a binomial model with a stock with starting price of \$100. Each period the stock can go up 5% or drop 3%. An investment bank sells for \$0.80 a European call option on the stock that matures after five periods and has a strike price of \$120. Interest rate per period is 2%. Describe the steps to be taken by the investment bank in order to start hedging this short position at the moment the option is sold.

Solution: In order to find the hedge at the moment the option is sold we need to find the prices of the option after one period. In order to do that we also need to recover the risk-neutral probability. We observe that for the option to be in the money after five periods the stock has to go up all five periods (because $S(0)u^4d < 120$). The payoff would be

$$(1.05)^5 \cdot 100 - 120 = 7.63$$

We retrieve the risk-neutral probability from the formula,

$$p^* = \frac{1 + r - d}{u - d} = \frac{1 + 0.02 - 0.97}{1.05 - 0.97} = 0.625$$

We now compute the value of the option after one period. If the stock goes down the value is zero, because all the subsequent values are zero. If the stock goes up (to 105) the value of the option is

$$C^u(1) = \frac{1}{(1 + r)^4}(p^*)^4 7.63 = \frac{1}{1.02^4}(0.625^4)7.63 = 1.075$$

Now we compute the hedge as the solution to

$$\delta_1 105 + 1.02\delta_0 = 1.075$$
$$\delta_1 97 + 1.02\delta_0 = 0$$

with the solution $\delta_1 = 0.1344$ (the number of shares of the stock to buy) and $\delta_0 = -12.783$ (the amount to borrow from the bank). The cost of this position is lower than the price the bank is charging, so the bank can do the hedge while keeping a margin profit.

† **12.** In the previous problem suppose that another option with the same maturity is available with the Black-Scholes price given by the function

$$c(t, s) = s^3 e^{6(T-t)} \ .$$

If you still hold 10 units of the first option, how many options of the second type and how many shares of the stock would you buy or sell to make a portfolio both delta neutral and gamma-neutral (gamma equal to zero)?

Solution: Let us denote by x the number of the options of second type, and by y the number of shares of stock. Then we need the first and the second derivatives of the portfolio with respect to s to be zero, which means we have to solve the system

$$20se^{2(T-t)} + 3xs^2e^{6(T-t)} + y = 0$$

$$20e^{2(T-t)} + 6xse^{6(T-t)} = 0$$

Solving this system we get

$$x = -\frac{10e^{4(T-t)}}{3s} = -2.463, \quad y = 14,297.6595$$

† 20. The Black-Scholes price of a three-month European call with strike price 100 on a stock that trades at 95 is 1.33, and its delta is 0.3. The price of a three-month pure discount risk-free bond (nominal 100) is 99. You sell the option for 1.50 and hedge your position. One month later (the hedge has not been adjusted), the price of the stock is 97, the market price of the call is 1.41, and its delta is 0.36. You liquidate the portfolio (buy the call and undo the hedge). Assume a constant risk-free interest rate and compute the net profit or loss resulting from the trade.

Solution: In order to hedge the short position in the call we replicate a long call. Since the initial delta is 0.3, we start by buying 0.3 shares of the stock for $0.3 \cdot 95 = 28.5$ for which we need to we borrow a total of $28.5 - 1.33 = 27.17$. We deposit the margin $1.50 - 1.33$ in the bank. We next compute the constant continuous interest rate from

$$99 = 100e^{-0.25r}$$

with solution $r = 4.02\%$. The value of our hedging portfolio one month later is

$$0.3 \cdot 97 - 27.17e^{0.0402 \cdot \frac{1}{12}} = 1.84$$

We buy the call for 1.41. Our total return is

$$(1.50 - 1.33)e^{0.0402 \cdot \frac{1}{12}} + 1.84 - 1.41 = 0.60 \quad .$$

10 BOND HEDGING

2. Prove Proposition 10.1.

Solution: Since the yields of all the bonds are the same and equal to r, so is the yield of the portfolio P. Its duration is then equal to, denoting by c_{ij} the i—the coupon of bond j,

$$\frac{1}{P}\sum_i i\frac{\alpha_j \sum_j c_{ij}}{(1+r)^i} = \frac{1}{P}\sum_j \frac{\alpha_j \sum_i i c_{ij}}{(1+r)^i} = \frac{1}{P}\sum_j \alpha_j P_j \frac{1}{P_j}\frac{\sum_i i c_{ij}}{(1+r)^i} = \frac{1}{P}\sum_j \alpha_j P_j D_j$$

where D_j is the duration of bond j.

† 6. Suppose that the annual interest rate is 4%. You have a liability with a nominal value of $300, and the payment will take place in two years. Construct the duration-immunizing portfolio that trades in two pure discount bonds: a one-year pure-discount bond with nominal value $100 and a three-year pure-discount bond with nominal value $100.

a. How many units of each bond should the portfolio hold?

b. If the rate drops to 3.5% after one year, is the value of all your positions at that time positive or negative? How much is it exactly?

Solution: *a.* The value of the debt is

$$\frac{300}{1.04^2} = 277.37$$

with duration 2. The price of the one-year pure discount bond is

$$P_1 = \frac{100}{1.04} = 96.15$$

with duration 1. Finally, the price of the three-year pure discount bond is

$$P_3 = \frac{100}{1.04^2} = 88.90$$

with duration 3. In order to immunize our position, we have to allocate $ 277.37 between the two pure discount bonds, in proportions α and $1 - \alpha$ respectively, such that

$$\alpha + 3(1 - \alpha) = 2$$

with solutions $\alpha = 0.5$, $1 - \alpha = 0.5$., that is, we invest $0.5 \cdot 277.37 = 138.68$ in each bond. We, then, buy $138.68/96.15 = 1.442$ units of the one-year bond and $138.68/88.9 = 1.56$ units of the three-year bond.

b. The value of our liability is now

$$\frac{300}{1.035} = 289.855$$

With respect to the value of our assets, on one hand we have the cash value of our holdings in the one-year bond that has just matured, equal to $1.442 \cdot 100 = 144.2$. On the other hand we have 1.56 units of the other bond, which is now a two year bond, with price

$$\frac{100}{1.035^2} = 93.35$$

for a total value of the assets of $144.2 + 1.56 \cdot 93.35 = 289.858$. The value of our position is (barely) positive, equal to 289.858-289.855=0.003.

† **8.** Consider a zero-coupon bond with nominal $100 and annual yield of 5%, with one year to maturity. You believe that after one week the yield will change from 5% to 5.5%. Find the expected change in the bond price in three ways:

a. Exactly, computing the new price

b. Approximately, using the initial duration

c. Approximately, using the initial duration and convexity

Solution:

$$\text{a.} \quad \Delta P = \frac{100}{1 + 0.055} - \frac{100}{1 + 0.05} = -0.4514$$

$$\text{b.} \quad \Delta P \approx -\frac{D}{1+y}P\Delta y = -\frac{1}{1+0.05}95.2381 \cdot (0.055 - 0.05) = -0.4535$$

$$\text{c.} \quad \frac{\partial^2 P}{\partial y^2} = T(T+1)\frac{100}{(1+0.05)^{T+2}} = 172.7675$$

and thus convexity is $C = 172.7675/95.2381 = 1.8141$. We get

$$\Delta P \approx -\frac{D}{1+y}P\Delta y + \frac{1}{2}CP(\Delta y)^2 = -0.4535 + 0.0022 = -0.4513$$

11 NUMERICAL METHODS

† 2. The one-year spot rate is 6%. According to your model of the term structure you simulate the values of the one-year spot interest rate that could prevail in the market one year from now. You do only five simulations and get 6%, 6.52%, 6.32%, 5.93%, and 6.41%. Compute, using Monte Carlo, the rough approximation of the price of a one year European call on the two-year pure discount bond with strike price 94.

Solution: The possible prices of the two-year bond one year from today are given by $P = \frac{100}{1+r}$. This gives the values 94.3397, 93.8791, 94.0557, 94.4012, 93.9761. The payoffs for the call are, respectively, 0.3399, 0, 0.0557, 0.4012, 0. The average is $(0.3399 + 0 + 0.0557 + 0.4012 + 0)/5 = 0.1595$. The present value, which gives us the estimate for the price of the call, is $0.1595/1.06 = 0.1504$.

† 8. Why do you think it is not easy to apply the Monte Carlo method to compute prices of American options?

Solution: The price of an American option is a maximum over random maturities of the corresponding European payoffs. Thus, it is a maximum of a huge number of expectations. With Monte Carlo we can easily compute one, or several expectations and compare them to see which one is the largest, but it is not that easy to compute the maximum of infinitely many expectations. In general, it is not easy to use simulation for solving optimization problems.

† **12.** Explain why expression (11.14) is the continuous-time version of expression (11.13), and find the Black-Scholes formula for the call option on the continuous geometric mean (11.14).

Solution: Denoting the geometric mean by G, We have

$$\log(G) = \frac{1}{n} \sum_{i=1}^{n} \log(S(t_i))$$

For large n this is approximated by $\frac{1}{T} \int_0^T \log(S(u)) du$. Next, we have

$$\log(S(t)) = \log(S(0)) + (r - \sigma^2/2)t + \sigma W(t)$$

and thus

$$\frac{1}{T} \int_0^T \log(S(u)) du = \log(S(0)) + (r - \sigma^2/2)\frac{T}{2} + \frac{\sigma}{T}[TW(T) - \int_0^T t dW(t)]$$

We see that the continuous geometric average G_c is lognormally distributed. Consequently, we can use the regular Black-Scholes formula for the price of the call option at time $t = 0$, except in the expressions for d_1, d_2 we replace rT with $\log(E[G/S(0)])$, and $\sigma^2 T$ with

53

$Var[\log(G)]$, because for the stock price we have $\log(E[S(T)/S(0)]) = rT$ and $Var[\log(S(T))] = \sigma^2 T$, and its lognormal distribution is completely determined with these quantities. We now compute those. First, by Stochastic Calculus, we have

$$\text{Cov}[W(T), \int_0^T t\, dW(t)] = E[\int_0^T dW(t) \int_0^T t\, dW(t)] = E[\int_0^T t\, dt] = T^2/2.$$

Thus, we have

$$Var[\log(G_c)] = \sigma^2 \left\{ T + \frac{1}{T^2} \int_0^T t^2\, dt - \frac{2}{T} \text{Cov}[W(T), \int_0^T t\, dW(t)] \right\} = \frac{\sigma^2 T}{3}$$

Also, using the fact that for a random variable X with normal distribution $N(0, \gamma^2)$ we have $E[e^{aX}] = e^{\frac{a^2\gamma^2}{2}}$, we get

$$\log(E[G_c]) = \log(S(0)) + (r - \sigma^2/2)\frac{T}{2} + \frac{\sigma^2 T}{6}$$

$\dagger^{**}$ **18.** Use the retrieval of volatility method to find the initial value of the optimal portfolio for maximizing the expected log-utility of terminal wealth $E[\log(X^{x,\pi}(T))]$, in the Black-Scholes model, with any parameters you wish to choose. Compare to the exact analytic solution derived in chapter 4.

Solution: You can use a formula given in section 11.2.6. For the log utility we have $I(z) = 1/z$ and $\hat{\lambda} = 1/x$. You can simulate $Z(T)$ under risk-neutral probability from

$$Z(T) = e^{-\theta W^*(T) + \frac{\theta^2}{2}T}$$

where $\theta = \frac{\mu - r}{\sigma}$. The analytic formula for the optimal portfolio is $\hat{\pi} = \frac{\theta}{\sigma}X$.

† **2.** Recompute all the examples in section 12.1 with the log utility replaced by the exponential utility $U(x) = 1 - e^{-ax}$.

Solution: We first consider the case of one agent in a single-period setting with two consumption goods. The maximization problem is given by

$$\max_{\{c_1, c_2\}} \left\{ \alpha(1 - e^{-ac_1}) + (1 - \alpha)(1 - e^{-ac_2}) \right\}$$

such that

$$P_1 c_1 + P_2 c_2 = X \ .$$

Solving for c_2 and substituting in the previous expression, we get

$$\max_{\{c_1, c_2\}} \left\{ \alpha(1 - e^{-ac_1}) + (1 - \alpha)(1 - e^{a \frac{X - P_1 c_1}{P_2}}) \right\}$$

The optimal solution is

$$\hat{c}_1 = \frac{aX + P_2 \log \frac{1-\alpha}{\alpha} \frac{P_2}{P_1}}{aP_1 + aP_2}$$

$$\hat{c}_2 = \frac{aX - P_1 \log \frac{1-\alpha}{\alpha} \frac{P_2}{P_1}}{aP_1 + aP_2}$$

and the equilibrium prices are the solutions $\hat{P}_1$ and $\hat{P}_2$ to the following nonlinear system:

$$Q_1 = \frac{aX + P_2 \log \frac{1-\alpha}{\alpha} \frac{P_2}{P_1}}{aP_1 + aP_2}$$

$$Q_2 = \frac{aX - P_1 \log \frac{1-\alpha}{\alpha} \frac{P_2}{P_1}}{aP_1 + aP_2}$$

Consider now a case of two agents, with utility functions

$$\max_{\{c_1^A, c_2^A\}} \left\{ \alpha(1 - e^{-ac_1^A}) + (1 - \alpha)(1 - e^{-ac_2^A}) \right\}, \quad \max_{\{c_1^B, c_2^B\}} \left\{ \beta(1 - e^{-ac_1^B}) + (1 - \beta)(1 - e^{-ac_2^B}) \right\}$$

We assume that they are endowed with consumption goods, e_1^i, e_2^i, for $i = A, B$, and their wealth is, then, given by

$$W^i = P_1 e_1^i + P_2 e_2^i, \ i = A, B$$

From Walras' Law we know that if one of the two consumption good markets is in equilibrium, the second consumption market is also in equilibrium. Then, we only consider equilibrium in the first consumption good market, $\hat{c}_1^A + \hat{c}_1^B = e_1^A + e_1^B$. This implies that equilibrium prices result from solving

$$\frac{aX^A + P_2 \log \frac{1-\alpha}{\alpha} \frac{P_2}{P_1}}{aP_1 + aP_2} + \frac{aX^B + P_2 \log \frac{1-\beta}{\beta} \frac{P_2}{P_1}}{aP_1 + aP_2} = e_1^A + e_1^B$$

Since

$$X^i = P_2 \left(\frac{P_1}{P_2} e_1^i + e_2^i \right), \ i = A, B$$

We can rewrite the equilibrium condition as

$$\frac{aP_2 \left(\frac{P_1}{P_2} e_1^A + e_2^A \right) + P_2 \log \frac{1-\alpha}{\alpha} \frac{P_2}{P_1}}{aP_1 + aP_2} + \frac{aP_2 \left(\frac{P_1}{P_2} e_1^B + e_2^B \right) + P_2 \log \frac{1-\beta}{\beta} \frac{P_2}{P_1}}{aP_1 + aP_2} = e_1^A + e_1^B$$

Dividing numerator and denominator of both terms of the left hand-side by P_2 we can rewrite the equilibrium condition as

$$\frac{a \left(\frac{P_1}{P_2} e_1^A + e_2^A \right) + \log \frac{1-\alpha}{\alpha} / \frac{P_1}{P_2}}{a \left(\frac{P_1}{P_2} + 1 \right)} + \frac{a \left(\frac{P_1}{P_2} e_1^B + e_2^B \right) + \log \frac{1-\beta}{\beta} / \frac{P_1}{P_2}}{a \left(\frac{P_1}{P_2} + 1 \right)} = e_1^A + e_1^B$$

This is an equation in the ratio of prices P_1/P_2 and its solution gives us the equilibrium relation of prices.

We now consider the two-period problem. Suppose that the optimization problems of the two individuals, A and B, in this economy are given as

$$\max_{\{c^A(0), c^A(1)\}} \left\{ (1 - e^{-ac(0)^A} + \alpha(1 - e^{-ac(1)^A} \right\},$$

$$\max_{\{c^B(0), c^B(1)\}} \left\{ (1 - e^{-ac(0)^B} + \alpha(1 - e^{-ac(1)^B} \right\},$$

where $0 < \alpha, \beta < 1$. The investors are endowed with amounts $e^i(j)$ of the good, where i is the individual and j the time at which they receive the endowment. In order to simplify, we use the consumption good as numeraire and normalize its price to 1 at each period (we can think of the consumption good as money). The budget constraints of the individuals are given by

$$c^i(1) = e^i(1) + [e^i(0) - c^i(0)](1 + r), \quad i = A, B .$$

Substituting the budget constraint in the utility function of the individuals, and using optimality conditions we get

$$c^A(0) = \frac{1}{a(2+r)} \left[\log \left(\frac{1}{\alpha(1+r)} \right) + a(e^A(1) + e^A(0)(1+r)) \right]$$

$$c^B(0) = \frac{1}{a(2+r)} \left[\log \left(\frac{1}{\beta(1+r)} \right) + a(e^B(1) + e^B(0)(1+r)) \right]$$

From the equilibrium conditions $c^A(j) + c^B(j) = e^A(j) + e^B(j)$ (which, by the budget constraints, also imply that the bond market clears), we derive that the equilibrium interest rate is the solution to the following non-linear equation,

$$\frac{1}{a(2+r)} \left[\log\left(\frac{1}{\alpha(1+r)}\right) + a(e^A(1) + e^A(0)(1+r)) \right]$$
$$+ \frac{1}{a(2+r)} \left[\log\left(\frac{1}{\beta(1+r)}\right) + a(e^B(1) + e^B(0)(1+r)) \right] = e^A(0) + e^B(0)$$

Finally, we consider the case of uncertainty about the futures states. There is a single agent that tries to solve

$$\max_{\{c(0),c(1)\}} \left\{ (1 - e^{-ac(0)}) + \beta E[1 - e^{-ac(1)}] \right\}$$

where the uncertainty is caused by the endowment process of the agent. We assume that $e(0)$ is known, while at moment $t = 1$ there are two possible states, 1 and 2, with probabilites p and $1 - p$. The random endowment $e(1)$ is $e_u(1)$ in the state 1 and $e_d(1)$ in the state 2. The budget constraint of the agent is

$$c_i(1) = (e(0) - c(0))(1 + r) + e_i(1) , \quad i = u, d ,$$

where i represents the state. The objective function of the individual becomes

$$\max_{\{c(0),c(1)\}} \left\{ (1 - e^{-ac(0)}) \right.$$
$$\left. + \beta \left[p(1 - e^{-a[(c(0)-c(0))(1+r)+e_u(1)]}) + (1 - p)(1 - e^{-u[(e(0)-c(0))(1+r)+e_d(1)]}) \right] \right\}$$

At time $t = 0$ the optimal consumption of the agent has to be equal to the endowment, $\hat{c}(0) = e(0)$. This, together with the budget constraint guarantees that the investment in the bond market is zero. Substituting $\hat{c}(0) = e(0)$ in the optimality condition, we derive the equilibrium interest rate

$$1 + r = \frac{e^{-ae(0)}}{\beta \left[pe^{-ae_u(1)} + (1 - p)e^{-ae_d(1)} \right]}$$

13 CAPM

† **2.** In a CAPM market, the expected return of the market portfolio is 20%, and the risk-free rate is 7%. The market standard deviation is 40%. If you wish to have an expected return of 30%, what standard deviation should you be willing to tolerate? How would you attempt to achieve this if you had $100.00 to invest? (Remark: short-selling is allowed.)

Solution: By CAPM we have $\mu_i = R + \beta_i(\mu_M - R)$, and thus, we need to have

$$0.3 = 0.07 + \beta_i(0.2 - 0.07)$$

with solution $\beta_i = 1.77$. We want to hold an efficient portfolio, and, therefore, it has to be on the capital market line, hence

$$\sigma_i = \sigma_M \frac{\mu_i - R}{\mu_M - R} = 0.7077$$

The minimum standard deviation we would have to be willing to accept is 70.77%.

† **4.** Suppose that we estimate the standard deviation of a portfolio P to be 10%, the covariance between P and the market portfolio to be 0.00576, and the standard deviation of the market portfolio to be 8%. Find the idiosyncratic risk of P.

Solution: We first have to compute the beta of P,

$$\beta_P = \frac{\sigma_{PM}}{\sigma_M^2} = \frac{0.00576}{0.08^2} = 0.9$$

We also know that the total risk of P, σ_P, is

$$\sigma_i^2 = \beta_i^2 \sigma_M^2 + \sigma_\epsilon^2$$

or

$$(0.1)^2 = (0.9)^2(0.08)^2 + \sigma_\epsilon^2$$

with solution $\sigma_\epsilon = 6.94\%$.

† **6.** The expected return and standard deviation of the market portfolio are 8% and 12%, respectively. The expected return of security A is 6%. The standard deviation of security B is 18%, and its specific risk is $(10\%)^2$. A portfolio that invests $\frac{1}{3}$ of its value in A and $\frac{2}{3}$ in B has a beta of 1. What are the risk-free rate and the expected return of B according to the CAPM?

Solution: We can derive β_B from

$$\sigma_B^2 = \beta_B^2 \sigma_M^2 + \sigma_\epsilon^2$$

59

or

$$(0.18)^2 = \beta_B^2(0.12)^2 + (0.1)^2$$

with solution $\beta_B = 1.25$. Now, we can compute β_A from

$$\frac{1}{3}\beta_A + \frac{2}{3} \cdot 1.25 = 1$$

with solution $\beta_A = 0.5$. We get the risk-free rate R from the CAPM formula

$$0.06 = R + 0.5(0.08 - R)$$

with solution $R = 4\%$. We can get now the expected return of B, also from the CAPM formula, as

$$\mu_B = 0.04 + 1.25(0.08 - 0.04) = 0.09$$

† 10. The risk-free rate, average return of portfolio P and average return of the market portfolio are, respectively, 4%, 8%, and 8%. The estimated standard deviation of the market portfolio is 12%, and the estimated nonsystematic risk of portfolio P is 15%. The Jensen index for portfolio P is 1%. What can you say about the performance of portfolio P?

Solution: The Jensen Index indicates, in principle, how good the performance of a portfolio is. Since for this portfolio it is positive, the perfomance seems to be good. However, we will compute the Treynor and the Sharpe Indexes as well. In order to do that, we need to know the beta and the standard deviation of portfolio P. From the definition of the Jensen Index we can compute the beta:

$$0.01 = 0.08 - (0.04 + \beta_P(0.08 - 0.04))$$

with solution $\beta_P = 0.75$. We can now derive the standard deviation from

$$\sigma_P^2 = \beta_P^2\sigma_M^2 + \sigma_\epsilon^2 = 0.75^2 0.12^2 + 0.15^2 = 0.0306$$

with solution $\sigma_P = 17.5\%$. The Treynor Index and the Sharpe Index are, then,

$$T = \frac{0.04}{0.75} = 0.05; \ S = \frac{0.04}{0.175} = 0.23$$

The Treynor index of the market is 0.04 and its Sharpe index is $0.04/0.12 = 0.33$. That tells us that this portfolio shows a relatively good performance when we consider the market risk, but a poorer performance when we consider its total risk. It is probably a good portfolio to be held as part of a larger portfolio, but not a good single investment.